Policing by Multi-Racial Consent
The Handsworth Experience

Policing by Multi-Racial Consent

The Handsworth Experience

John Brown

BEDFORD SQUARE PRESS | NCVO

This edition published 1982 by the
Bedford Square Press of the
National Council for Voluntary Organisations
26 Bedford Square London WC1B 3HU

'Shades of Grey' appeared as a Cranfield Institute study 1977

ISBN 0 7199 1087 0

Typeset by D. P. Media Limited, Hitchin, Hertfordshire

Printed and bound in England by
The Whitefriars Press, London and Tonbridge

Contents

'Black and white are proportionally bad as well as proportionally good, living under the same conditions and environment of our imperfect civilization.'

Marcus Garvey, *The Philosophy and Opinions of Marcus Garvey* (1967)

'The vast majority of residents of *any* community, black, white or brown, will turn out to be not only law-abiding but also possibly law-assisting. My job, the job of any patrol officer, is to enlist the law-abiding allies in the struggle against crime and criminals.'

Patrick V. Murphy and Thomas Plate, *Commissioner* (1977)

'Good policing will be of no avail, unless we also tackle and eliminate basic flaws in our society.'

The Brixton Disorders 10–12 April 1981, Report of an Inquiry by the Rt Hon the Lord Scarman

Foreword

The Rt Hon the Lord Scarman PC

Future historians may well say that the nation's battle for policing a multi-racial society by consent was won on the Soho Road and in the backstreets of Handsworth. It is too soon to cry victory or stage a triumphal march: but, if Sir Philip Knights' principles and David Webb's practice outlive their respective periods of office as Chief Constable and as police officer in command at Thornhill Road, victory should be assured.

The evidence of what has so far been achieved, the thinking behind it, and the lessons for future action, are on record, largely thanks to John Brown and the Cranfield Institute. In 'Shades of Grey' (a Cranfield Policy Study, 1977) he brought Handsworth into prominence, putting on record the work being done there by the people and their leaders as well as by the police. Now he re-visits Handsworth, reports progress and some failures, and gives us his assessment of the chances of achieving a genuine consensual basis for the policing of multi-racial communities.

My experience has taught me two fundamental truths. The first is that successful policing depends upon our tackling and eliminating basic flaws in society. Currently the basic flaw is a compound of racial disadvantage and racial prejudice. This truth has to be learnt, and the appropriate cutting-out operation devised and carried out, by society as a whole: by all of us.

The second truth does relate primarily to policing methods. I would simply repeat what I said in paragraph 9.2 of the Brixton Report (Cmnd 8427; Penguin Books, 1982):

'[The police] are not responsible for the disadvantages of the ethnic minorities. Yet their role is critical. If their policing is such that it can be seen to be the application to our new society of the traditional principles of British policing, the risk of unrest will diminish and the prospect of approval by all responsible elements in our ethnically diverse society will be the greater.'

Unfortunately, the police cannot wait for us to get society right. They are on duty now: and in the inner city as well as in the country. They must act swiftly and effectively to suppress public disorder, protect life and property, and enforce the law. The Handsworth experience, faithfully and vividly told by John Brown in this book, reveals the devastating awkwardness of the police dilemma. Have they a way through? Are they to stand inevitably condemned – by some as ineffective or by others as oppressive?

Handsworth points to a conclusion, which I suspect many policemen are reluctant to accept. Success will come, only if the police take the initiative. They have to go out into the community and talk – talk about their operations and their problems as well as about anodyne (but valuable) things like football, social events, club activities, and winning the interest and confidence of the children. This is not easy, as the uncertain history of the Lozells project (Chapter 8) shows. If people feel that they are the objects of an imposed police benevolence, they will turn away. But, if the people see the police as co-operating in their ventures and activities, mutual trust can develop.

I confess that the most disturbing feature, which John Brown wisely does not conceal from us, is that many policemen do not accept the central importance of 'community relations', as sadly the basic British principle of policing by consent has come to be called. They are, I believe, the victims of the technological myth. They appear to think that technological advance is the true professionalism of the police. They mistake the part for the whole. Technology has enhanced the speed and efficiency of police response to disorder and crime. But the police have a preventive role: and in a multi-racial society prevention is less likely to cause anger, resentment, and loss of confidence than response to a situation after the event. The police must be professional: but their profession, now as always, has to include the philosophy and the practice of 'the bobby on the beat'.

This is a timely book. It is practical and thoughtful. John Brown has provided us with the evidence. Do we accept it, and act upon it? Or do we reject it? Our survival as a civilised community depends upon our answer.

Scarman
26 September 1982

Preface

Growing concern in Handsworth about relationships between police and black youth led Anthony Wilson (Secretary of the Barrow and Geraldine E. Cadbury Trust) to suggest that I visit the area in May 1977 to talk both with local critics of the West Midlands Police and with the Chief Constable, Philip Knights (now Sir Philip Knights). Thereafter I was asked to make a short study of policing in the area which would focus on police–West Indian relations there, and if possible, offer 'constructive proposals' in this sphere.

Having shared the experience of West Indians in a number of Caribbean Islands, and the experience of police in a number of English forces, I did not expect the issues to be simple: black versus white; law and order versus deviance and disorder; oppressors versus victims. Realities are usually more complex than the perspectives of political, racial or professional ideologies; and Handsworth proved no exception.

I found, for example, that relations between Handsworth police and first generation West Indian settlers were, in general, far more benign than most critics would allow; and that conflict was centred on relations between the sections of police mainly responsible for local 'contact' policing – in particular, young CID and young uniform officers – and the sections of West Indian youth mainly responsible for the crimes of greatest local concern – street robbery and theft from the person – many of them alienated from their own families as well as from white society, and seeking identity in a Rastafarian guise.

In certain ways, the young blacks and the young blues

mirrored each other. Each a minority group under pressure, uncertain of themselves, and looking to identify with their group culture. Each prone to take on the style, habits and perspectives of their tribe, and with them its prejudices and myths. Each tense and expectant of threat from the other. Each liable to cover insecurity with aggression, to be too hasty in word, gesture, judgement, act. Each now harassing, now harassed. Victim or oppressors? Which was which?

If the conflict seemed riddled with double visions, ambiguities, 'Shades of Grey', in some measure it also seemed inevitable. For many young West Indians, the police were so much more than enforcers of the law, keepers of the peace. They personified 'Babylon': all that is racist, unjust, oppressive, unacceptable.[1] As for the young coppers who had shared the experience of victims of local street crime, and who knew something of its real – that is to say, human – meaning, the physical and psychological damage it does, the fears and the trauma it breeds, it was difficult for them not to identify those mainly responsible – young West Indians – with violence and criminality of the worst kind.

What, then, to propose? Independent, detailed investigation of specific cases of reported police violence against West Indians – and equally, of reported West Indian violence against police – would clearly help to disentangle fact from myth at one level of conflict. Yet it would be hard to achieve; to find appropriate investigators; to gain trust and co-operation to follow through enquiries. And even then, at the end of all, how acceptable and influential would, or could, the findings be in a climate so subject to suspicion and distortion? Could they act as springboards for remedial action, or would they only serve to harden existing polarities, justify further conflict?

In doubt of this, I aimed my main proposals to tackle causes rather than symptoms of conflict. And since local police-community problems were so plainly influenced by the local context of economic and social disadvantage, it seemed imperative to set my proposals for improvements in policing strategy in a wider social policy context. In terms of police practice, I thought the primary need was to improve the quality of 'contact' policing by augmenting the uniform strength on the ground (then 20 per cent under strength, more than half the patrol constables being probationers with less than two years' service) with officers of greater experience, i.e. less liable to over- or under-react under stress, and more liable to exercise that most precious of police powers, discretion.

A second priority was to provide more locally responsive police coverage, particularly in the critical areas to the south and east of the sub-division, by giving greater emphasis to foot patrols, and by leavening the strength of the permanent beat police officers with younger men able and willing to extend contact with schools, community groups, neighbourhood associations and other social agencies, so mobilising local capability for self-regulation. Such measures could also serve to close the gap between foot and car patrols, and to bring the preventive and reactive roles of the police into more effective relationship.

Beyond these, the main task, as I saw it, was to associate the resources of the police more closely with those of other social agencies, and with local community resources, to make common front against the vexed and taxing problems of care and order which confront them all. A vital lead in creating networks of understanding and collaboration had already been given by the newly appointed sub-division Commander, Superintendent David Webb,* enabling police and community to prevent escalations of conflict and disorder – for example, during the African Liberation Day celebrations in Handsworth Park (June 1977) – thus creating new trust and confidence in police purposes.

These initiatives pointed the value of preventive strategies that could offer the youth most at risk creative alternatives to disaffection and criminality through improved employment, work experience, educational, cultural and recreational

---

* Superintendent Webb was appointed as Commander of Handsworth sub-division in June 1977, having served there as Chief Inspector from January 1976.

opportunities. I thought that such strategies would be the more credible and effective if they could involve as many as possible of those agencies – statutory and voluntary – whose work relates to the needs and problems of local youth; and suggested, amongst other things, that a club which could offer young people a wide range of the opportunities outlined above might form a useful base for collaborative action.

Responses to 'Shades of Grey' were, to say the least, varied. At one end of the spectrum, the consultation draft of the Birmingham Inner City Partnership programme (1980–83) commented that it 'has proved very helpful and the recommendations, where they applied to the police force, have been implemented'. In fact, the Chief Constable of the West Midlands Police, reinforced the Handsworth sub-division strength with twenty experienced constables in January 1978 to improve the quality of contact policing, and in 1979, in collaboration with the West Midlands Education, Probation and Social Services, and with the backing of Inner City Partnership funds, launched a major community policing project in the Lozells area of Handsworth – the Lozells Project.*

Amongst those who view the scene from ideological perspectives, political or racial, the report found little favour; but few criticisms were as harsh as those of Rex and Tomlinson in their study of *Colonial Immigrants in a British City: A Class Analysis*.[2] 'Shades of Grey', they commented, 'can only have the effect of directing the police and any extra legal group which chooses, to use violence against an easily recognisable minority, whilst possibly failing to actively prevent the growth of crime.'

What, then, are the realities of policing in Handsworth? In what directions is it moving? Towards greater community contact and involvement, or towards repression and oppression? In particular, what have been the effects of police policy and practice on police–West Indian relations in Handsworth over the four years between 1977 and 1981? Given the var-

---

* For the Lozells Project – see also pages 107–10.

iance of the interpretations, it seemed worthwhile to take fresh soundings, attempt further analysis, of these issues in what has become a key test area for police and society.

This book is thus in two parts. First is the original report – 'Shades of Grey' – which came from sharing the experience of police and policed during July 1977. Second is 'Handsworth Revisited', the product of many visits between 1977 and 1981, in particular during the two years up to and including the riots of 1981.

The main purposes of the book are to convey something of the 'touch and feel' of policing in Handsworth, and to explore some of the underlying issues confronting police and society in the aftermath of the riots and the subsequent Inquiry of Lord Scarman. Many contributed to those purposes: Anthony Wilson, whose invitation set the study in motion; Sir Philip Knights, who gave me *carte blanche* to nose and question where and when I wanted; the officers of Thornhill Road Police Station, to whose understanding, experience and open dealing I owe so much; and people of all conditions – blacks, browns, whites and blues – met and talked with at all hours in pubs, clubs, temples, churches, cells, cafés, shops, squats, schools, offices and private houses, as well as in the park and on the streets, over several years.

I would like them to know how grateful I am to them; and how deeply the sights, sounds, smells of Handsworth, and the lively mingling of its peoples, are embedded, with affection, in my mind.

John Brown
Handsworth – Golant – Cranfield
1977–82

Part I
Shades of Grey: Police–West Indian Relations in Handsworth

1 The Problem Area

Local crime data

Handsworth forms part of the C1 sub-division of the West Midlands Police, and in terms of crime statistics, the record of C division is unremarkable amongst the twelve divisions of the force. In the first four months of 1977, it ranked tenth in recorded crime, eighth in detected crime, and was the only division with a fall in crime against the same period of the preceding year. Yet in cases of robbery and assault with intent to rob, it led the field, and also ranked fourth in its incidence of thefts from the person.

The C1 sub-divisional perspective brings the nature of local crime into more significant focus. The sub-divisional area with its component beats is shown on page 4. Its reported crime statistics for the year ending 30 June 1977 are given on page 5.

For the local public, the incidence of street robberies and thefts is of particular concern, as is the nature of the assailants and victims. The main facts here are, firstly, that some 90 per cent of the known assailants are youths of West Indian origin or descent; secondly, that the great majority of the known victims are the defenceless – mainly women and the elderly. Most of the known victims are white, though recent representations to the police by the local Asian community indicate that the number of Asian victims of such crimes is a good deal more significant than reported in the crime statistics, and that the comparative reluctance of Asians to report crime tends in turn to make them favoured targets. In Handsworth there is thus more than usual cause for reservations about the validity

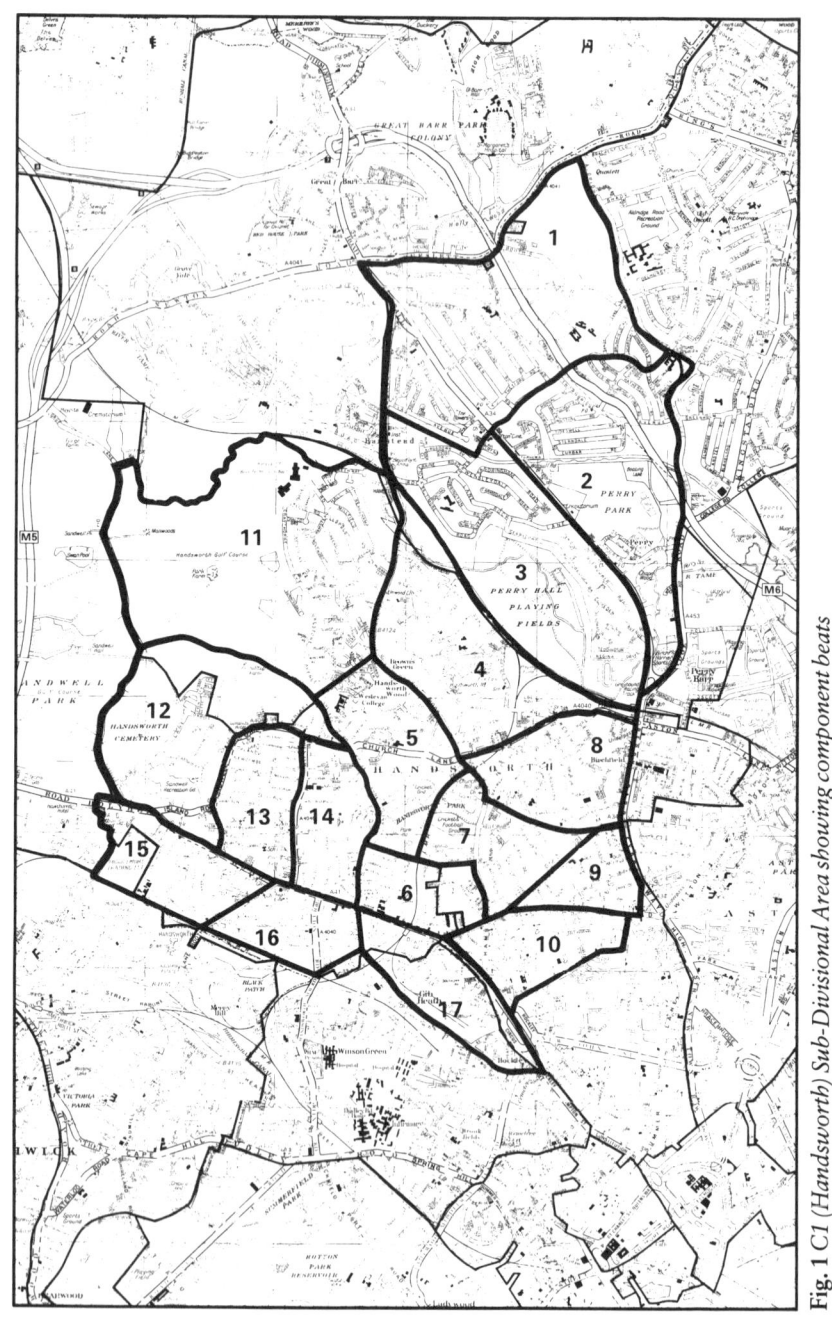

Fig. 1 C1 (Handsworth) Sub-Divisional Area showing component beats

Reported crimes committed on the Handsworth Sub-Division between 1 July 1976 and 30 June 1977

	Robbery Theft from the Person	Burglary		Woundings Assaults	Indecency Offences	Theft from Shops	Theft Pedal Cycles	Other Thefts	Motor Vehicles			Criminal Damage	Other Crimes	Totals
		D/H	O/B						Theft of	U/T	Theft From			
July	15	101	65	21	2	12	25	61	96	11	37	29	33	508
Aug	21	58	90	13	5	15	22	57	83	12	22	18	31	447
Sept	17	92	66	10	1	13	11	75	77	12	19	14	30	437
Oct	31	87	81	24	2	22	13	66	76	17	25	22	32	498
Nov	20	92	82	21	4	5	12	70	86	19	27	25	21	484
Dec	11	60	50	16	5	11	1	45	77	9	27	16	31	359
Jan	10	92	67	19	2	10	7	54	103	15	32	28	29	468
Feb	15	64	76	16	2	7	1	58	98	21	16	26	21	421
Mar	23	93	89	15	4	16	11	80	95	9	32	26	35	528
April	16	126	92	18	3	8	25	68	90	17	27	35	24	549
May	19	97	101	30	6	5	26	82	81	17	28	27	22	541
June	17	108	81	10	8	9	24	74	87	11	38	41	21	529
Totals	215	1070	940	213	44	133	178	790	1049	170	330	307	330	5769

D/H = Dwelling House; O/B = Other Building; U/T = Unauthorised Taking of crime statistics, and experience of the area makes it apparent that both for local people and for local police the realities of local crime are a good deal more serious than statistics suggest.

These realities vary considerably even within the sub-division, and the main areas of concern can only be defined by relating analysis of sub-divisional crime records to the working experience of officers on the ground. It then becomes clear that the most serious police problems relate to crimes of violence against persons and personal property – notably robbery, thefts from the person, burglary, woundings and assaults; mainly committed in a particular area of C1 sub-division – comprising beats 6, 7, 8, 9 and 10 and parts of beats 5 and 17; mainly at particular times – between dusk and the early hours of the morning; mainly by a particular group – some 200 youths of West Indian origin or descent who have taken on the appearance of followers of the Rastafarian faith by plaiting their hair in locks and wearing green, gold and red woollen hats. The tragic irony is that whilst these youths claim identity as Rasta men, the nature of their criminality in fact represents a betrayal of the non-violent ideology of the Rastafarian faith; and in view of the concern expressed on this score by brothers of the Ethiopian Orthodox Church, it is appropriate to make distinctions between true Rastafarians and the criminalised Dreadlock sub-culture in Handsworth.

The critical area

The critical area is ringed on the map of Birmingham (page 7). Social contrasts are brutally juxtaposed within it. To the north, a few streets such as Wellesbourne Road, of quiet affluence: neat houses and gardens adorned with hanging baskets, conifers, flowering shrubs, roses in bloom, well-kept lately registered cars on driveways – a reminder of Handsworth's past as a county borough. Yet turn out of Wellesbourne Road into Church Hill Road, walk east, and as you go, social disadvantage and physical dereliction rapidly gather about you. Turn south then, to Lozells Road and the streets

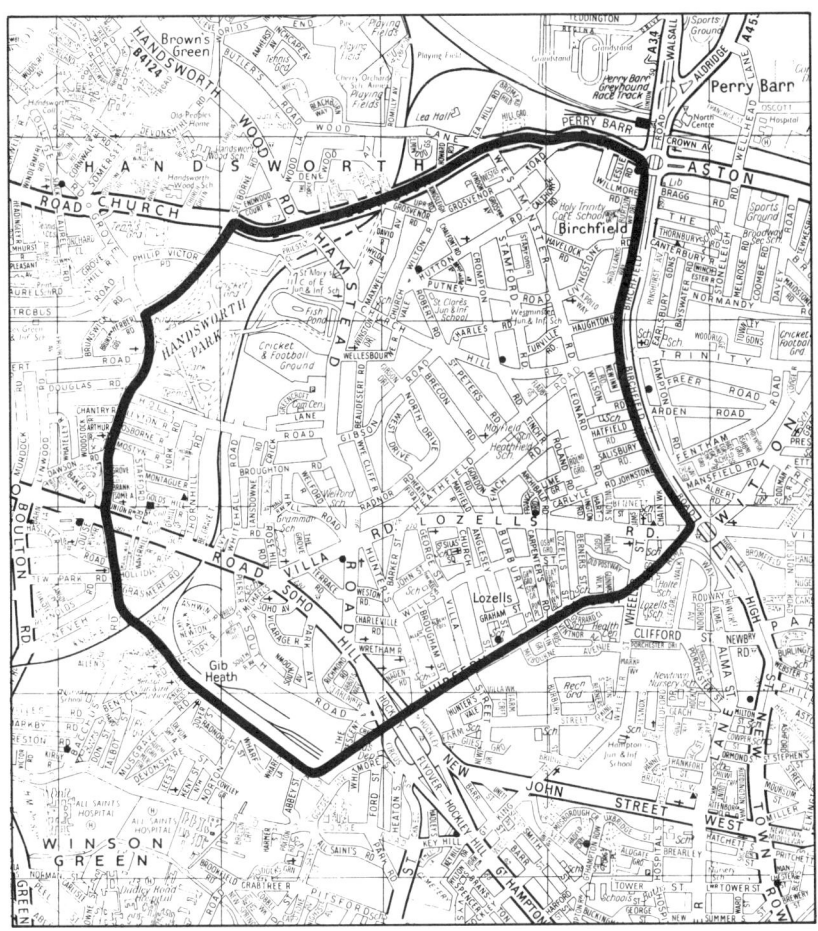

Fig. 2 *The critical area*

beyond, amongst a growing number of shuttered or shattered houses – 'like bad teeth', as the local beat officer describes them – and you feel here the true pulse of Handsworth, the sense of a district sliding inexorably into physical and psychological decline. For overall, Handsworth is of crucial concern both to police and society: a key test area where problems of immigrant settlement, youth and age, deprivation, unemployment and housing stress meet and compound each other in an exacting context of urban decay.

The critical area covers a great deal, though not all, of the Handsworth and Soho wards. Latest estimates from the Central Statistical Office in Birmingham – on its own advice, to be treated with caution – give the two wards a total population of 48,000. This included 12,400 (26 per cent) of Asian stock (5,400 British-born) and 12,700 (26.5 per cent) of West Indian stock (5,700 British-born). These are almost certainly under-estimates, and in particular they do not adequately reflect either the density of the local West Indian youth population or the fact that the majority of these youth are of Jamaican origin or descent.

Of an estimated local working population of 38,000 – based on an area comprising, but greater than, the two wards – 4,615 (3,438 males, 1,177 females) were registered as unemployed at the most recent count (12 May 1977): an official unemployment rate of 12.2 per cent. Those of West Indian stock made up 1,067 (23.1 per cent) of the total number of registered unemployed – 740 males and 327 females.* (They also represented one-third of local school-leavers in July 1977.) Yet once again official statistics are an inadequate guide to the heart of the matter: the growing numbers on the local ground of unemployed West Indian youth. Their presence is conspicuous on the streets: often they gather on the pavements outside the houses or squats they occupy (currently

---

* 955 were registered at employment offices, 112 at careers offices, but distinctions of this kind now lack real significance, since registrations may be made at either office.

26 on the sub-division), in such numbers such as to make very credible community workers' estimates that well over 25 per cent of local West Indian youth are currently unemployed (1977).

These West Indian youth are certainly amongst those most poorly equipped for employment. Many of the Dreadlocks with whom I spoke, in squats, on the streets, in the area housing office and in the sub-divisional (Thornhill Road) police station, have suffered from schooling split between vastly differing educational regimes in the West Indies – mainly Jamaica – and in Britain, and have records of poor educational attainment. Many also have records of poor family relationships, and have either rejected, or been rejected from, their homes. Deprived and disadvantaged, they see themselves as victims of white racist society, and attracted by values and life style of alienated Dreadlock groups, drift into lives of idleness and crime, justifying themselves with half-digested gobbets of Rastafarian philosophy.

Many of the couple of hundred 'hard-core' Dreadlocks who now form a criminalised sub-culture in the area live in squats. Almost all are unemployed. And apart from the specific crimes for which they are responsible, they constantly threaten the peace of individual citizens, black, brown and white, whilst making the police task both difficult and dangerous, since every police contact with them involves the risk of confrontation or violence. Moreover, they exert growing influence on several hundred other West Indian youth on their fringe, whose numbers swell as more of their kind leave school with records of limited attainment in an adverse employment context. In this way, more and more young people of West Indian stock are put at risk; and the influence of the criminal sub-culture also extends out into the community, where more and more people grow fearful not only of reporting crime but also of giving information or evidence that could lead to the arrest or imprisonment of the malefactors. Thus statistics of reported crime become ever less accurate as reflections of local police problems.

The police sub-division

The local sub-divisional force functions from Thornhill Road Police Station. Built in 1883, when it also functioned as a Police Court, it preserves the looks and smells of a Victorian institution, musty with sweat and polish and accumulations of police experience. Downstairs it is an echoing maze of corridors and improvised offices, some separated by plasterboard, much of it lit by ancient strip lighting. Upstairs is usurped by a huge vaulted cavernous room, the CID (Criminal Investigation Department) office, reminiscent of an old West Indian schoolroom or general store. Some of its ornamented windows are still shattered from the siege last year by local West Indian youth. And it is a moot point as to who complains most about the station, the black youth who constantly curse it as the fount and origin of police oppression or the young police who constantly curse its 'diabolical amenities'. But there it is – for the Dreadlocks, the brick and stone heart of 'Babylon',* and for the people of the area as a whole, so oddly monumental a symbol of policing that some have even made representations to the police to preserve it as sub-divisional headquarters.

In its staffing, the sub-division reflects the problems of the West Midlands force as a whole, i.e. a current 10 per cent deficiency in strength allied to growing wastage and turnover rates. In July 1977, the deficiency in uniformed officer strength was, in fact, nearer to 20 per cent than to the force average.

---

* 'Babylon' signifies both the oppressive systems of established society and the police as enforcers of the laws that maintain the society.

2 Police Functions

Work of the uniform branch units

The essential task of the uniform branch is the patrolling function, by car or on foot. It also supplies officers for attachments ranging from Crown Courts to the CID. The main strength is deployed in 4 units providing 3 shift coverage (06.00 – 14.00 hrs; 14.00 – 22.00 hrs; 22.00 – 06.00 hrs) of the 17 sub-divisional beats backed by 9 panda cars (an allotment based on 1 car per 2 beats). Each unit is commanded by an inspector, with 4 sergeants and a complement of constables which in July 1977 was: Unit A – 24; B – 23; C – 23; D – 21. Of these, three or four from each unit are likely to be on leave or sick or on courses at any one time.

It is the constables on the units who deal with almost all the incidents on the ground. Their deployment, in car or on foot, is determined in general by their inspector, but the way in which they are used in response to specific incidents is directed primarily by the unit sergeant who functions as controller. He is linked by personal radio with all unit officers, by computer with force headquarters; has access to the national police computer for information on stolen cars; and handles all calls from the public. In determining the nature and priorities of police responses to local incidents, he is a key figure, making decisions from a firm basis of experience.

'If I know one person can deal with an incident, I send a foot patrol. If prompt action is needed, a mobile. But of course it depends a good deal on what calls are coming in and what resources are available. At times, not often, most of the mobiles are free. Other times, I'm stacking jobs. And it depends too on who's involved and where. Beats 6 to 10, crime's above average. That's the main West Indian area. And where Rastas are involved, there's always a risk of violence. Then I usually send more than one car, especially if a WPC's in it. Or at least have another car standing by . . . Over-reacting? I don't think so. I've seen too many of the lads done over. And I've suffered myself. Look, there's the scar still on my arm where a Rasta bit me last year. Right through the uniform.'

Apart from the deficiency in their numbers, the unit constables responsible for most local contact policing are characterised by their youth and comparative lack of experience. In A unit, in July 1977, 13 of the 24 were probationary constables (i.e. in their first two years of service); in B unit, 12 out of 23 were procons; in C unit, 13 out of 23; and in D unit, 10 out of 21 (an overall 53 per cent of procons). The average age and lengths of service of the unit officers were as follows:

A *unit*	Constables	Procons
	11	13
Average age	27	20½
Average service	6½ years	1 year
B *unit*	Constables	Procons
	11	12
Average age	25	19½
Average service	5¾ years	1 year
C *unit*	Constables	Procons
	10	13
Average age	27	20
Average service	6 years	1 year
D *unit*	Constables	Procons
	11	10
Average age	29	20
Average service	7 years	1 year

Of the constables, 11 of the 91 were women, 9 of them probationers. The average age of the two women constables was 22, that of the nine procons, 20. The youngest was 18½, a slim neat girl who had just completed her first week of service, on night duty. Two nights before I spoke with her, following a 999 call about the suspected unauthorised taking of a motor car, she had pursued suspects with two other officers, jumped a seven foot wall, and found a six foot Dreadlock coming at her. She dived and held him until the other two officers came up, subdued and arrested him after a violent struggle. So after her first week, she felt she belonged.

Such incidents are the commonplaces of the area. And the meaning of the police experience there can best be expressed by direct reference: the record over two days of the first unit officer with whom I had extended contact.

M is 22 with three years' service, all of it on the sub-division. He comes on duty at 1.45, Friday afternoon. We go out in a panda following reports of a stolen car being driven through the area. The reports fail, and we are redirected to a shabby terraced house where an Indian has just reported his car stolen. The family and the neighbours stand waiting on the pavement in silent desolation. The woman next door had caught sight of the man driving the car away, but she speaks only a few words of English. What did he look like? 'Small man. Jamaica man.' The two Indian men then interpret, evoking precious few details. We all go inside. The little boy and girl of the house begin to cry. Wide-eyed, the mother comforts them. All stand helpless in the bare room, looking at M. He gathers what information he can; gives some words of comfort and reassurance. Back in the car, he reports in. 'It's quiet this afternoon, just for a while at least. Yesterday this time we were rushed off our feet . . .' So he signals out, to drive me over the ground.

Impressions of place and people grow into patterns: of abrupt transitions from red-brick affluence to gutted desolation; of street upon street going to seed; of ageing whites, particularly old ladies with bowed backs, tired faces, thin shopping bags; of busy Indians, their ladies in smart saris, opening more shops in the Soho Road; of knots of young West Indians against broken fences, shouting abuse and jerking fingers as the panda passes.

We talk as we go: of how the area continues to deteriorate since he began his service, since I was last here; of how unemployment, youth crime, violence grow; of how pressures mount on police whilst they rely more and more on inexperienced procons. M reckons the percentage of procons on the station has quadrupled over three years.

'They rely on them far too much now. As for the young women police constables, it's just impossible to use them here on equal terms, whatever the new Act says. The risks and threats of violence are just too great. The old system where they had their own separate role, that was much better. No wonder so many women now are leaving the service . . . Me, I accept the dangers of the job. You either accept it or you don't do it. And I like the constant activity, the action, the pressures. The pressures make a close-knit community. All of us at Thornhill Road, we have to rely on each other. So there's this sense of comradeship. Even relationships between the ranks are easy. All of us, we're always busy. Too busy for many formalities. All in it together . . .

As for crime, it's almost all local. We get few big jobs or organised crime by outsiders, like you might get in Sutton Coldfield. The worst of it here is West Indian. It's nothing to do with the colour, though. I don't believe I'm prejudiced like that. What I hate is thieves . . . Most of the older West Indians I know, they're no trouble. The trouble's the young ones, say 10 to 25 . . . To my mind the trouble begins and ends in the homes. West Indians seem to have just two approaches. Either too much discipline, so their kids rebel and kick out on their own. Or too little, when the kids do just what they like . . . And it's not just the boys. The girls are often more vicious, stirring the boys to violence, and violent themselves. We've just had three cases of assault by girls. A copper hit with a steam iron. Another attacked with a knife. The third kicked in the testicles. Put him off duty for two weeks.'

M has been attacked himself a number of times, twice badly assaulted. The previous Guy Fawkes Day in Handsworth Park, whilst chasing a suspect, he was set on by a group of West Indian youth, knocked down, and twelve of them stood round and kicked him unconscious. He was in hospital for two weeks. The other time he came upon some West Indian youths burgling a house. 'I chased them into the garden. Suddenly they stopped and turned on me. Next thing I knew they'd knocked me down and were kicking me all round the garden . . .'

A call comes in – a complaint by an old couple of youths on the street outside, shouting, playing football, causing a disturbance. The old man suffers from acute bronchitis and bad nerves. His wife says that if he dies, it will be at the youths' door. They cause him constant distress with their noise. M goes out to the bunch of young West Indians on the street: tells them they must play fair; asks them to understand the old people's plight: 'You've got to live with the people next door, haven't you?' If they want a game, there's spaces nearby, away from the houses. After the telling off, an awkward joke or two passes between the kids. One shoves another. The other makes as if to do him over. M feels the boy's muscle. 'There's nothing there, is there? More fat on a greasy chip.' All laugh. The tension is over. We move off.

Then stop by a building site. Kids run away. Pipes and brickwork smashed up. Movement within a half-built house. M runs to find a middle-aged West Indian couple there, also concerned to chase away vandals. 'They're always at it here,' M says. 'Criminal damage. But what can you prove? If you catch them at it, maybe you can have them for five quid's worth of damage. But what would that mean in court? It's not likely to get past the Superintendent.'

Off to a call from some old people's cottages. Another complaint of disturbance by children playing. M catches two of them as they run off. Whites, eleven or twelve years old, well-tended and well-heeled. They stand stiff to attention whilst M gives a stern warning: flushing with fear; eyes like organ stops. 'Next time I'll be round to your Dad's , and he'll clip your ear. Understand?' 'Yes, sir. Yes, sir.' And they bolt away.

M shrugs and smiles. Then spends a while reassuring the old lady who made the call. 'Old people are our best informants.

Often they've nothing else to do but to see what's going on outside their windows. And they like nothing better than to have a chat about how things aren't what they used to be. And they're right. They aren't. Least of all round here . . .'

So the common round of a quiet day continues. At ten o'clock M comes off duty, then puts in four hours' overtime on the anti-vandal patrol. During that time comes a 999 call of an Indian's house ransacked. Shortly afterwards, M and a colleague stop a car with the suspects in it – three whites and a black. They detain and arrest them. Guns and knives are found in the car, including a meat cleaver some three feet long, with a fifteen inch wide blade. It seems the four had gone to the house with intent to murder. M is relieved they all come quietly, and books them for aggravated burglary. The time he's through, it's 6.00 a.m. Saturday morning.

Back on duty at 1.45 p.m., Saturday afternoon. Then out on patrol. At 4.00 p.m., whilst I sit with the Sergeant Controller, comes a call reporting the theft of a car wheel by four West Indian youths; then almost immediately M radios in that he has stopped the suspect car and requires assistance. The Controller calls up three more pandas '. . . just in case. M's on his own. There could be violence and they'll need a few men to sort it out and bring in the suspects.' Between calls he checks the number of the suspects' car on the national computer. (There have been 1,049 thefts and 107 unauthorised takings of motor vehicles on the sub-division over the past year.) The car is reported as having collided with a cemetery wall some months back; nothing more.

The four suspects are brought in, put into separate rooms. The eldest has a strong, hard, intelligent face, the usual green, gold and red woollen hat, a pale blue pullover, trousers rolled up to his calves, worn running shoes. He immediately accuses M of picking on blacks. M rounds on him. 'Don't start that business with me. We've got you here not because you're black but because you're accused of nicking a wheel. I don't care if you're black, white, green or have two horns on your head.' He goes off to collect the complainant, leaving an office constable in charge of the youth. 'Eh, what's all the fuss, man? All you need do is call the scrap yard, check on the wheel there. Just one phone call. And the whole thing cleared up.' 'That's what we're doing, checking up,' says the constable.

For a few moments the youth sits with his dreadlocked head on his hands between his knees. Then looks up. 'I just want to save you paperwork,' he says, with all the concern of one who has been here before and knows the routine. 'Just one phone call. Soon put it right . . .' Pause. 'You're held on suspicion pending enquiries,' says the constable drily. 'So let's have your property out on the table.' 'Eh, what you taking my property for?' The constable says nothing, begins to fill in a form. The youth slowly puts down dark glasses, keys, lighter, hat, rasta belt. 'I'd like to see the Chief Constable.' 'I'm only here to take details,' the constable says. 'Name?' Name: Earl Rowe.* Age: 20. Born Jamaica, 1956. Came to this country, 1966 . . .

I leave to see the complainant, Mr C, a small island man, a motor mechanic in working overalls. During the morning, he'd been working on cars at the small garage back of his house. In the afternoon he'd come out to find a young lad sitting in one of the cars he'd left parked in the roadway. He was sure he'd locked it. The lad said he'd found the door open. Some minutes later he noticed the car had its off rear wheel missing. Then saw the young lad and three other youths by a car they had parked near by, now fitted with the steel rimmed wheel from his own car.

> 'I say to them, look, all I want is me wheel back. Just give it back and I forget all about it. I wouldn't want to cause the kids trouble just for a tyre. All they had to do was to say okay Mr C, here is your tyre. Then it all finish. But the tall one, all he would do was to give me abuse. So at last I say, look, I go call the police. Then they drove the car off. Had to push-start it though.'

He describes the four suspects. Yes, he would know them again. Especially the young one who'd sat in his car. 'He could

---

* All names of suspects given here are fictitious.

hardly have left school.' He repeats he didn't want to get the kids into trouble. If only they hadn't abused him. He shakes his head. 'Why do kids behave this way?' 'Why then?' I ask. He scratches his head, thinks the law is partly to blame. In the West Indies, parents are allowed to discipline the kids. Here, if you beat them, the police or the social services can take you to law. So parents can't discipline kids like they used to at home.

Home, I discovered, is the village below where I lived on the same island. Mr C smiles wide with delight. We talk small island matters. But what of the police here? Does he think they harass West Indian kids? He has no experience of it. But then, he's had little or no contact with police here . . . He reads and signs the statement M has written out; and M drives him home.

Suspect No. 2 is Winston Richards: tough, square, muscular. Age: 18. Born Jamaica. Came to this country: 1966. He rattles off the exact date like clockwork. He has done so many times before. Left school at 14. Has never worked. Draws £11.35 a week social security. Lives in a squat. 'When I came out of Borstal, right, I had a chance to go home, right. I said no . . . Now all I'm waiting for is to go out of here.' 'Who took the wheel?' 'It wasn't me.' 'One of you, wasn't it?' 'Yeah, one of them. Don't know who. It wasn't me, right. So all I'm waiting for, right, is for him, right, to say who did it. Then I go out of here . . .'

Whilst M is interviewing the others, Winston tells me, quite dispassionately, of the jobs he's done. Since he was 12, he's been in permanent trouble. First, stealing from cars. Then theft from the person, burglary, robbery, obstructing police, criminal damage. A few months back he threw a youth employment officer through the window of the local careers office. At present he's on licence from Borstal and on two years' probation. Ten previous convictions. Yes, he knows the time of decision is coming. So what will he do? Well, when he left Borstal last year (the date again to the day), he decided not to get in trouble again. Though he knows how difficult that is if opportunity knocks. 'What do you really want then?' 'I want a permanent place to live, right. Everyone should have his own place to live.' 'And work?' 'Yeah. When I was in borstal I learnt motor mechanics, right. City and Guilds standard. Next September, right, I put down for college.' M comes back. 'I want to talk to you next.' 'I hope you make it,' I say, as Winston goes out of the room. The young probationer constable who's been taking the personal details looks at me. 'He's honest, that one, I reckon.' He shrugs and sighs.

Suspect No. 3, tall and slim. Name: Rex Wynter. Age: 18½. Came to this country, 1969. On bail to Crown Court for theft. 'A regular attender. Twice a year man,' says the duty Inspector. Had instruction as a welder. Hasn't worked since 1974. Like the first two, on £11.35 a week social security. Refuses to make a statement.

Suspect No. 4, the youngest, stands doe-eyed, mute. To name, age, address, he shakes his head. The police doubt if he's even 16. Whilst they talk, two Dreadlocks come to the front desk, both sharply dressed, the biggest very handsome with a black peaked cap over his locks. 'I've come for the boy Paul Anthony,' he says. 'I'm his protector. He's only 15.' 'I knew it', the duty Inspector tells M. 'He's under age. You'll have to put him in the Detention Room.' He explains the legal position to the youths at the front deck: that the boy can only be released to parents or guardian. 'He has no parents. He's in my care. I'm responsible for him.' 'But not in law,' the Inspector says. 'And if there's no parent or guardian, we have to inform the social services.' 'But I've been a social worker, part-time, with Harambee.' 'Afraid that's not good enough, old son.' The two youths leave. Enquiries are made about the boy. 'Poor little sod,' the Inspector comments later. 'Seems that when he was three his Dad got killed in a traffic accident. His Mum died the year after. He's been in care ever since. Last April he absconded from an assessment home . . .'

M's questioning yields little. Winston Richards makes a voluntary statement, saying that he saw others take the wheel and admitted that he withheld this information from the owner when challenged. The others refuse to make statements, to be photographed or to be fingerprinted.* Towards ten o'clock, M and a Detective Constable go to the cells to interview Rowe again. Wynter calls out: 'I want a word with you.' As the CID man enters his cell, Wynter shouts, 'Watch out. You're going to get killed', and strikes him. As M intervenes, Wynter seizes him round the neck, punches his face, and pushes his fingers into his eyes, gouging at them. After a struggle, Wynter is subdued and locked in again. When M returns to duty at 1.45 p.m. on Sunday afternoon, he reports sick from the effects of the assault and fatigue.

Next day at lunch time, I visit M at the local police hostel. He has bruised eyes, a cut ear, bruises about the body. 'But I feel better now. Slept more than twelve hours together. Be back on duty in a day or two.' Wynter meanwhile is charged not only with theft but also with assault on a police officer and with the damage or destruction of the Detective Constable's watch, under the Criminal Damage Act. When charged, he answers 'Fuck off.' All in all, an incident which cannot but reinforce the local animosities of both young blacks and young blues. And all for a tyre; even for the West Indian owner, a matter of little or no importance.

M returns to duty later that week, and by Friday has made four more arrests. 'Twelve in a week, that's my record.' Case-hardened, confident, decisive, young men like him are not easily deterred. But for the young women constables on the unit, the difficulties are greater, the issues more complex, and their views on their own role much more ambiguous, swaying between commitment and awareness of their own limitations, between enthusiasm and fear.

Y sums up the situation: a woman probationary constable, neat and charming, aged 20, with just over a year's service, all at Thornhill Road, and rated by all 'a good kid'. 'I love the job. But I don't think we women have a role here. Often I think we're quite useless. At best we can only be used in restricted

---

* A court order for these procedures was finally applied for, but the application was withdrawn at the last moment when the accused gave way.

ways; and when there's real violence, what can we do?'

On foot patrol, the young women on the units operate on or near the main roads only, and never on their own after 6.00 p.m. On car patrol, they rarely go out in pairs, and never without a male colleague after dark. Y and her colleagues take threats Dreadlocks have made very seriously.

'They've said they'll take a WPC, gangbang her and return the bits to Thornhill Road . . . I've been followed by groups of Rastas out on patrol, and involved in incidents that really frighten me. It's made me wonder how long I can continue. And the policeman I'm, well, almost engaged to, he wants me out, at least from this kind of job in this kind of area.

The worst time was one night in mid-May. This crowd of young West Indians were trying to get into a club on the Soho Road. It was full, and the manager wouldn't let them in. This led to a disturbance and a 999 call. The mobiles and the anti-vandal patrol were called out. And as we got there, a fight started and the crowd rushed to join in. They threw bottles and coke tins full of stones at the police. That's why we thought later that some had come prepared . . . I stood back, on the fringe of it all. Then I saw this Rasta by a wall, waving a bottle about, screaming obscenities at me, and I was frightened. I turned to get away behind a transit van. As I turned, he threw the bottle at me. It smashed at my feet and gashed my leg open. Anyway they collected me up and took me off to hospital. My leg needed four stitches. And on top of all that, I was told off for being out of the car. They said I should have stopped in the car to attend the radio. But it would have been just as dangerous there.'

'And I started to ask myself then, what is our function? All this talk of equal status, it's nonsense here. There's no way a woman constable can do the same job as a man . . . Even in silly, small details. Take this job yesterday. A 999 call. Report of kids nicking stuff from a void house. When we got there, two white boys were running away up an entry, and as we went after them I couldn't run fast enough to catch up with the one I was after, and you know why? This skirt we have, it's too tight to run in properly . . . But the boy stopped, so I was able to arrest him. But only because he stopped of his own accord . . . As for the protection we have, the woman's truncheon, it's a complete waste of time. Mine's at home in a drawer.'

'On the one hand I'm moaning about the problems here. But I wouldn't work anywhere else. I fought to come back here. And I'm glad I came back here. To work here is marvellous. The blokes are really great . . . And out on the beat, like 10 beat, that's my favourite, there's this tremendous mix: West Indian, Asian, English, Irish . . . And you see too that the blacks there are not all the same. You need to see that. Because in this job, you sometimes get to feel that there's not good and bad, but just bad. And that isn't true.'

The air of Handsworth, it seems, is full of contradictions. Beyond those evoked in Y's mind by her local experience are those evoked by – or imposed upon – almost every incident which involved young Dreads and young police. The incident that put Y and six other police officers into hospital,* for example, had been cited to me at the end of May as a classic example of police 'stupidity and high-handedness'; a case of innocent black youth subject to intolerable 'harassment' and reacting under stress to resist and fight back against it. The facts as I found them do not support such a black and white interpretation. In particular it seems clear that it was a 999 call reporting disturbance outside the Monte Carlo club (at the junction of Soho and Villa Road) which led to the police presence there just after midnight on Sunday, 15 May 1977;

---

* Thirty-five sub-divisional officers, two of them women police, were injured as a result of assaults during the year ending 30 June 1977. These numbers mounted dramatically in August 1977 as a result of political violence during the Ladywood parliamentary by-election.

and that the disturbance appeared to derive from the frustrations of some fifty to seventy young West Indians unable to get into the club. Moreover, it is a fact on record that the man who threw the bottle at Y – and who failed to answer the charges in court during the time of my visit – had a record of ten previous convictions, including possession of an offensive weapon, larceny, theft and wounding with intent. And the most vicious assault that night was almost certainly committed by a 6 foot 4 inch Dreadlock with a record of fourteen previous convictions, including indecent assault, burglary, assault occasioning actual bodily harm, criminal damage and the possession of an offensive weapon. He stabbed a policeman in the knee with a 20 inch long knife, after which the policeman used his truncheon to ward off more blows. There are about twelve cuts across the truncheon, some of them quite deep . . . In brief, as I looked at the record, black and white interpretations assumed shades of grey. But amid the contradictions of Handsworth, one matter is sure: in the ranks of those of all colours who suffer harassment are the young police on the units.

Work of the permanent beat officers

But those officers represent only one face of the police in Handsworth. Another, very different, face is represented by the sixteen Permanent Beat Officers, each of whom is responsible for one beat of the sub-division, beats 12 and 13 being covered by one officer. Administratively, the PBOs are shown as attached to the four units, but the differences between them and the other unit officers reveal themselves in terms of age; length of service; function; perception of the job; attitudes to and relationships with the public; and even to some extent in terms of character and values.

Where the average service of the unit officer is 3 years, that of the PBOs is about 15 years, the junior PBO (something of an exception) having 3 years' and the senior 26 years' service. Such differences do not make for very close working relationships. The young men on the units tend to be dismissive of the PBOs' operational role, seeing it as a fringe activity to the real action, rather as fighting troops view the role of those in the back lines. On their side, the PBOs see the unit officers as dashing from incident to incident unable to give them the attention, understanding, judgement and 'follow-through' that they merit. There is substance in both sets of criticism.

On foot on a beat of your own, perspectives diverge from those of panda drivers. The people that you see on streets, in shops, schools, pubs, clubs, churches, trades, local associations, voluntary and statutory services, etc. over time become known to you more and more as individuals rather than as social or racial stereotypes. As that local personal knowledge extends, so your capacity grows to fit attitudes and actions to circumstance; to discriminate between what is and what seems to be; knowing why, where and when to encourage or admonish, to wave the stick or wink the eye; in a word, how to exercise that most precious of police powers, discretion.

And where the concern of panda drivers tends to centre on the particular moments of particular incidents, the PBO perspectives tend to be long term. The people he has dealings with are those he will see again tomorrow and again after tomorrow, whom he knows will continually assess and reassess his attitudes and his actions amongst them, and adjust their measure of confidence and co-operation accordingly. He is thus more directly and permanently accountable to them than are the men in the pandas; and his effectiveness is much more deeply rooted in the quality of his local relationships. In this sense the PBO comes nearer in function to the original concept of the constable in the English police tradition.

Perspectives differ in other, related ways. Whilst the primary object of a PBO relates closely to Sir Richard Mayne's definition of fundamental police functions – 'the prevention of crime . . . the protection of life and property, the preservation of public tranquillity' – the essential purpose of the panda system is to respond to criminality and disorder. Each approach evokes a distinct concept of the police function, the 'preventive' involving wide human and social perspectives, the 'reactive', much more specific job-oriented perspectives.

Out on the ground, the distinctive approach of the PBOs

becomes immediately apparent. 'I regard myself as a civvy doing the job of a policeman,' says one officer. Like others amongst his colleagues, much of his concern centres on the roots of local problems, the quality of local housing, playing facilities, schooling,* employment, family life. This is hardly surprising, particularly on those beats in the critical area marked on the map (see page 7), where the sense of deprivation and dereliction is often overwhelming. Walking the foot-beat, the 'feel' of the area comes home both in physical terms – the terraced streets strewn with litter and broken glass, the eyeless houses, rundown shops, crumbling façades – and in terms of the conflicting human experience within it.

Conflict particularly surrounds the houses and squats occupied by Dreadlocks. 'I can see their problem,' says one PBO.

> 'No one wants to know them. Many of their parents won't have anything to do with them. Once they get into trouble two or three times, that's it . . . So they find places in the squats. There's five main Rasta squats on my beat now, maybe fifty or so kids in all. Numbers are never firm. They're always coming and going . . . But the pattern's growing. More kids in trouble, more houses left vacant as locals move out. And where they settle, then they're on the look-out for easy cash and food. So you find a rash of shoplifting, break-ins, burglary, robbery all round about, usually committed when cash or supplies run low.'

One squat on the beat is at the address given by Winston Richards at Thornhill Road Police Station. The PBO knocks at the door. 'What you want? Winston Richards, what you want him for? He ain't here.' Suddenly we are surrounded by Dreadlocks, questioning, shouting comments, waving arms. 'Winston Richards, I don't want him talk to you . . . You talk to him in the police station? Bet his lip all split, his face all swollen . . .

---

* The extent of PBO involvement in local schools is reflected by six requests from headmasters on the sub-division for local officers to accompany pupils on school camps during the summer of 1977.

No? Man, they does always beat up the blacks at Thornhill Road . . . But what you here for then? What you here for?' In the front is a thin scarfaced lad, brimming with aggression. 'This uniform, right, this police uniform, that is the uniforn of brutality, you understand?' 'But what about this man inside it, is he brutal?' 'That not the point, man. Don't you understand what I say? Understand, right. That is the uniform of brutality . . .' 'But uniforms can't harm you. Only men can. And is he, this officer here, personally brutal?'

They shy away from the subject. Once again, abstractions and ideological slogans refuse at the human fence. It is too threatening. They turn instead to the unseen police, particularly the CID at Thornhill Road. 'These people, man, I t'ink them nutty. Crazy men . . . That X and Y [naming certain CID officers] man, they is evil.' As they talk the Jamaican dialect is made thicker and thicker to assert identity and to repel outsiders. 'Dese X and Y, dis Sergeant Z, is fuckin animals. Break in the house, four in the morning. Turn the place over.' 'But didn't they have a warrant for someone's arrest?' 'Eh, we done nothin, we ain't t'ief, man. We is arl men of peace. Peace, dat is arl we look for.' As we walk away, the PBO takes a letter from a pocket. 'It arrived this morning. It's from the residents in this road. You'd better read it.'

Blank Road
Handsworth
Birmingham

Dear Sir,

Please could you do anything to help our neighbours and myself who are all being driven out of our minds with worry. There are these squatters in 'no. 17' who are making a thorough nuisance of themselves with radiogrammes blaring as loud as can be from morning till evening all the windows wideopen, then coming into the road intimidating anyone who would dare to say anything to them. They lean out of the windows watching every move so that we are afraid to leave our houses empty, we are afraid to come down our own road where many of us have lived all our lives. We get treated to displays of 'limbo' dancing in the road.

Surely we don't have to put up with this behaviour, even though we are told nothing can be done to get them out. We have phoned the police on numerous occasions but without results as of course these lads are 'crafty'. After causing a real rumpus in the road they then keep quiet for a short period before starting up again. Then invariably they are hanging out of the bedroom windows so naturally can see the 'panda' arriving.

Please, can you help us as we are all really very desperate. Everyone is talking about selling up but it is not always convenient to move and after all why should we because of about half a dozen wayward youths? I am not giving my exact address as if a panda car should call on us we are afraid of the consequences.

Please, please do something to help us. Desperate residents of Blank Road, Handsworth.

The smell of fear would not be as sour if this heart cry were not a representative voice. But the more I talked to people in the area, the more generally valid it seemed. The voice speaks for blacks as well as whites, though the fears of the ageing white residents are uppermost, since both their persons and their property are most at risk. And these fears intensify as locals become involved – however remotely – with any case relating to Dreadlocks. An off-licence owner, Mrs A, for example, witnessed some West Indian youths committing burglary nearby. As a result, she now finds herself with a notice to attend as witness at the Crown Court. Her attendance there will almost certainly be unnecessary, since a 'guilty' plea is entered; but she is desperately frightened, for Dreadlocks now hang about her shop, and have entered it knives in hand. She fears for herself and her livelihood; calls the police, feeling ever more menaced; wonders whether she can carry on or whether to give up the business.

The worries of the elderly are constantly heard over the counter of local shops, though their resentments are expressed rather against the specific causes of their fears – the young Dreads – than in blanket terms of colour or race prejudice.

(The time for prejudgment is long past in Handsworth: almost all judgments are post-experience.) 'We've got a family of Jamaicans next door. Lovely people. Do anything for you . . . The older West Indian people, they cause no trouble. And they themselves are ashamed of those young hooligans. If we'd had that lot on the Somme in 1918, we'd have shown them . . .'

People of other ages and backgrounds speak in similar terms – like Mrs P who was born in the district and returned three years ago to run a launderette:

> 'The middle-aged West Indians are easy to get on with, especially the women. They go out of their way not to offend. But the young people, they're very different. And over the last three years, I've seen how they've changed for the worse, into more aggression, more dishonesty. We've had young West Indian girls in here steal purses, mostly from Asian women. And the young men, shouting and pushing about, abrasive to everyone, me, the customers, even the Panda men when they've come in. Many of the middle-aged West Indians say they're terrified themselves by their own youngsters . . . You know, I came back here with very liberal views, but they're changing now.'

B, the PBO of the same area, also contrasts the two generations of West Indians:

> 'The first generation, you could always humour them, laugh and joke. Even for serious offences you could use humour. But those days are gone. The new generation questions everything. These Rastas, they're boys trying to seek identity, hostile to everyone. And what I'm afraid of now, it's the backlash it begins to create amongst the white youth.'

B is 38, with ten years' service, all but ten months of it at Thornhill Road. His beat covers some thirty streets in an area of major decline.

> 'Yes, it can be depressing, especially when you've been

away, say on holiday for a while, and come back and see it
again. Everywhere you look, there's problems – lack of
play space, youth clubs, places to meet. Everything's run
down . . . I'd like to spend more time with the people,
especially the juveniles. It takes time to build up relationships with them, especially those in trouble. Most of the
juveniles in trouble come from unstable or disturbed
homes. You've got to show you're willing to talk and
listen to them. Some of the Rastas, even, they're very
intelligent; a pleasure to talk to . . . But mostly there's too
little time. The beat's too big. I'm only scatching the
surface.'

The function of creating relationships with local groups and
organisations takes many shapes. Amongst the most promis-
ing are current initiatives for closer liaison between PBOs and
local residents' associations, strongly encouraged and aided by
Superintendent David Webb, deputy commander of the sub-
division from January 1976 to June 1977, and now appointed
to command. And there is little doubt that vigorous residents'
associations can play a major role in harnessing community
resources to preventive functions, particularly where they
bring settlers of different cultures and backgrounds together in
unity of local purpose.
  The Handsworth 1 Residents' Association, representing
people of some nine streets on the double beat 12/13, provides
a useful model. Of its 400 active members, about a third are
West Indians and Asians, and they are well represented on the
committee under an English secretary and a West Indian
chairman. In its work to improve both the local environment
and the well-being of local residents, it places considerable
value on the friendly involvement of the local – most junior –
PBO, and is ready to back police-community initiatives: 'the
police don't have enough assistance,' says the secretary. The
nucleus for further development is provided by the recent
formation of a youth section, which at the time of my visit had
some fourteen members, including five West Indians, under a
West Indian secretary and an English chairman.

Few other community groups and organisations in the area offer such an effective base for local action; and even in the critical area (beats 6–10) formal and informal residents' groups have been created: in July 1977, one on beat 6, two on beat 7, none on beat 8, two on beat 9 and one on beat 10. Some, at least, offer considerable potential for police liaison.

Yet overall, the work of the PBOs is beset with doubts and uncertainties, not least as to its status and priorities within the police function as a whole. The gulf between themselves and the other arms of the service is wide. And the PBOs here, as elsewhere, know that virtually throughout the service the myth that 'the most important man is the man on the beat' has long lost credibility. The most important man is so evidently the man with specialist rather than generalist functions. So that the permanent beat officers often think – and find – themselves at the bottom of the pile, with the lowest work priorities and regularly used as reserve stock. Local PBOs at Thornhill Road reckon to spend at least one day a week on office relief duties; and with further duties at matches and marches and one and one-half days' leave allowance, some three and one-half days a week are spent *off* the beat. Which gives limited time and scope to develop those understandings and working relationships through which community preventive action might be given effective focus and direction.

Work of the CID

At the other end of the spectrum, the third arm of the service, the CID, has neither the tendency nor time for doubt. Though in terms of service (detective constables average six to seven years) the CID stand between the unit officers and the PBOs, they relate more closely to the former in function and spirit. All is activity amongst them, their working atmosphere hectic. It is reflected even in their speed of speech, the pressures deriving not only from the incidence of local crime but from the nature of that crime and of offenders and victims as well as from the circumstances which characterise arrests and interrogations.

The special circumstances of CID work at Thornhill Road

particularly relate to the criminal activity and influence of the Dreadlock sub-culture. It is between the young Dreads and the younger CID officers that antagonisms are strongest, the potential for conflict greatest; the CID officers are named by Dreads as epitomising racist repression.

My own experience amongst CID officers at Thornhill Road left me in no doubt as to their strength of feeling against the criminal sub-culture, but I found little evidence of racist attitudes. Indeed some CID officers feel strongly that connections between crime and race in Handsworth are minimal. 'Of course our targets are mainly black. That's because most crime round here is committed by youths with black skins. And that's the point. Finally it's not a matter of race or colour or nationality but of generation. And the main fact for us is that most young people in Handsworth are black.'

Nor does race seem to affect the personal relationships of CID officers. Most of those with whom I had contact (those named by Dreads with most animus) do much of their eating in Indian cafes and their drinking in pubs with West Indian licensees, where their relationships – as I observed them – are both easy and cordial.

The longer I talked with local CID officers, the more clearly emerged the factors that shape their attitudes to the Dreads. These factors are the products of direct experience. Everywhere they go, to scenes of crime or disorder, they hear the same names, see the same faces. And the nature of the crime for which the Dreads and their followers are responsible can still shake even case-hardened detectives. Example: an 89-year-old man attacked at a bus stop by lads of 14, 13, 13 and 11. One of the boys involved had been committed the previous day to a community home for a robbery offence. In the evening he went out with three others, snatched a woman's handbag and spent the money in the centre of Birmingham. There they noticed the old man at a bus stop take out his wallet for his bus pass. They rode the bus with him to Handsworth, assaulted him as the bus moved away, stole several pounds from his wallet and dropped his glasses and pension book down a drain. They left him injured to spend the money in a cafe, and whilst the first lad returned to the community home, the others finished the evening smashing the windows of a Chinese restaurant.

Both CID and uniform officers were horrified by the old man's injuries:

> 'I saw him in hospital. Grand old bloke. Still conscious, chatting up the nurses. And I saw his leg. His knee-cap all shattered. The leg almost in two pieces. You could have put your fist in the hole between the pieces. And when I saw the kids who did it, so high, the youngest 11, I couldn't believe that kids that size could have done it.'

If there is a key factor in shaping police attitudes it is here. Often it is the police alone who see the real, i.e. human consequences of crime, which are frequently so much more than the physical or material damage assessed in the courts. They see constantly the pain and fear that persist after violence to people and property, know the nervous suffering and nightmares of victims, which may sour or blight whole lives, particularly those of the elderly. A senior detective in Handsworth put it thus: 'Everyone thinks about what should be done for the young. They ought to think more about what can be done for the older people – black and white – who suffer most from the crime round here.'

This factor – police concern for the victims – is too slightly regarded, too lightly considered, by society; and will continue so whilst political, legal and academic concern remains so obstinately offender-centred. Not until more effective attempts are made to see crime in the round – as a totality associating victim, offender and the full human consequences of crime – is society likely either to assess or to treat it realistically. To such attempts, police experience of victims can be of primary value and relevance.

Street robberies and thefts in Handsworth over the past year involved money and property ranging in value from nothing to £285. The most common item stolen was women's handbags. Often the losses in material terms were as trivial as the human losses were great. And beyond the personal, the family and the community losses, what value should be put, for instance, on walking the streets after dark without fear?

'The police are often accused of picking on black youth in the streets after dark. But if we stop anyone after dark, for whatever reason, like as not it will be a black youth. Who else is likely to be on the streets at that time? You've been here a while. Would you walk some of these streets after dark on your tod, out of choice?'

A current case in point is that of a woman going home at night, followed from the bus by three West Indian youths. In her statement to the police, she tells of one youth going in front of her, two staying behind. Then the one in front stops, turns, demands money. She gives them her handbag. They turn away, she thinks they are going, then they turn back. They demand more. She gives them £25 from a pocket. One youth then opens her coat, puts his hand inside her blouse. 'Please don't,' she says. 'I have three children.' She waits. They take money and the purse from her handbag, give the handbag back and leave her. It is a factual statement. One can only guess at her feelings at the time and at the after-effects of the experience on her.

Amongst other factors relating to Dreads that give growing concern to the CID are, firstly, that street robberies and thefts are increasing, as is the incidence of violence and the use of offensive weapons in their execution; secondly, that these crimes show signs of becoming more organised. Example: on 8 July, two West Indians operating from a stolen Cortina snatch a woman's handbag from behind. On 11 July, a similar offence is committed in a similar way by two West Indians operating from a stolen Capri. The two cars are subsequently found to be stolen at similar times within a few hundred yards of each other.

Thirdly, the influence of the criminal hard-core of youth is now increasingly felt amongst younger kids. More cases appear of schoolchildren involved in crime, even in 'muggings'. Example: a woman knocked over, punched in the stomach and her handbag snatched by school kids during school hours. Evidence also suggests that local youngsters now risk being drawn into organised theft, particularly of colour television sets, in which there is a thriving trade.

Fourthly, CID – and uniform – officers experience growing difficulties and dangers in making arrests and interrogating suspects. 'A main difference between young Rastas and others is that whilst the others usually co-operate after arrest, whatever they're like before, with the young Rastas you have to be prepared for aggro in one form or another – abuse, obstruction, lies, violence.'

Making an arrest can itself prove a risky business, in particular at Dreadlock squats. Officers with warrants for arrests may find themselves faced with barricades and may have to brave missiles, boiling liquids, offensive weapons. It is in such circumstances that dogs may be used. The dog van attends a good many incidents, since its very presence often deters disorder, yet dogs are brought out and used only in exceptional circumstances. They are greatly feared. Even police view them with some apprehension. 'During my five years' service, I've only seen them used three times,' a police constable tells me, 'and one of those times I was bitten myself. Still got the scar. And that was more than a year ago. There were twenty-five Rastas in this squat. We were trying to arrest some for burglary. Eight coppers and a dog. And they let the dog out and he bit me. Didn't bite one Rasta. Not one. Just me.'

Such resistance to arrest is compounded of many elements, the main ones being fear/hate and ideology. The fear is genuine and deep. Police officers themselves tell of youths, when arrested, shouting to their 'brothers', 'Don't let them take me. They'll kill me.' And in the squats, tales of police brutality are common currency which, through constant usage, are magnified into myth.

The ideology which feeds and feeds on this myth is an anomalous mixture, its components ranging from the philosophy and opinions of Marcus Garvey, Jamaican prophet of black nationhood, to current propaganda of the Socialist Workers' Party. (Garvey was strongly anti-communist and even flirted with Nazi concepts of racial purity during the 1930s.) Noble concepts of the dignity, worth and independent identity of black people mingle here with the vicious distortions of broadsheets like 'Flame'[3] which transposes the Handsworth police into brutal fascist racialist aggressors ('The Police are the *Real* Muggers') and the criminal sub-culture into black freedom fighters à la Soweto. In such ways the political far left seeks to make the Dreadlocks the tools of their class war. But in presenting them as legitimate heroes in the struggle against capitalism the far left at once encourages them to further personal violence and denies them their greatest need – policies and practice designed to remedy or redeem their damaged conditions of life.

The truth, I believe, is to be seen in human rather than political terms. The blues – plain-clothes or uniformed – with whom these blacks have most contact resemble them in that they too are young people under intense, often frightening, pressures. On the one side, the young Dreads, brimful of unused energies, fear and resentment, aggression and ideological ardour, some with violence aching to be out of them: a short fuse for any police sparks. On the other, the young coppers, understaffed, overworked, some on overtime (the young men with young families are those under greatest economic stress, and thus most likely to take it on), their noses constantly rubbed in the filth of human experience, the sufferings of Dreadlock victims, abuse, obstruction, lies; tense with expectations of meeting violence . . .

In such a context, it is not surprising if understanding and judgement are sometimes impaired, if violence sometimes ensues. From some mutual violence bitterness and myths develop on both sides. Almost inevitably – though still too hastily – police tend to identify Rastafarian appearance with unlawful force and criminality, despite the fact that the true adherents of the Rastafarian faith are often people of quietist disposition to whom crime is anathema. And police roughing up some youths – in whatever circumstances – create a permanent image of police brutality amongst the Dreadlock group as a whole, a myth sustained even when brutality is not encountered, since individuals exploit it as a means of asserting manhood and status within the group, and the group exploits it as a means of justifying further violence against 'Babylon'. In such ways myths absorb realities in Hndsworth; and in an atmosphere so thick with unsubstantiated accusations and counter-accusations, there is urgent need for an independent researcher or group of researchers to investigate in depth some of the allegations of brutality made against the police.

Despite polarisation between the two groups, CID officers see a few signs of hope: examples of Dreadlock youths returning from prison who prefer to drop out rather than return as leaders of criminality and disorder; and of youths who demonstrate violent hostility to the police within the group yet in private are ready to speak to them openly and without animus. In talking of such matters, detectives can reveal qualities of interest and concern which utterly confound accusations of racialism. What motivates them, above all else, is to *know* about people: 'Look here at these books we found at a Rasta squat . . . Swedenborg, *The Last Judgment*; *The Complete Home Carpenter*; *Feudalism and Modernization in Ethiopia*; *Who Am I? A Book of World Religions* . . . look what that shows about the lads there.'

It is on CID officers that pressures are greatest. As those most responsible for interrogating offenders and for preparing cases against them that may put them away, they are most threatened, both collectively and individually. Because of these threats, CID officers register their cars not at home addresses but at Thornhill Road. Some, like Z, feel the strain acutely. 'Some of these Rastas I've helped put down, they've told me, "We know your address, your phone number, your car number, who your family is" . . . Christ, if anything did happen to my wife and daughter, I'd go beserk.' After four years' service at Thornhill Road, he looks forward now to transfer, though not without regret, particularly for the companionship created there out of hard, shared experience.

Morale and relationships at Thornhill Road certainly command admiration; and because of, rather than despite, the pressures and conditions of work. Officers give an impression of people under fire, coping with adversity in conscious pride.

Something of a 'blitz' mentality pervades the station. 'If you can tackle Thornhill Road, you can eat any other station. You can tackle anything.' Variations of these words from a Detective Sergeant are constantly heard. 'I revel in it,' says a young detective. 'Going anywhere else would be like going out to graze on a farm.'

Here, perhaps, there are dangers too. No doubt this 'high' creates superb morale, but what are the costs of constant mainlining on adrenalin in terms of understanding, judgment? In brief, it may seem magnificent, but is it good policing?

3   Conflicts and issues

The potential for conflict

Realism is almost always there to temper commitment, however. Police experience is a great maker of hard heads, and supervisory officers on the sub-division have few illusions about the nature of the police task in Handsworth. They know the growing odds stacked against them by the economic and social context in which they work, and the extent to which that context determines the nature of their functions. So that virtually every form of contact with young Dreads, however remote from criminal matters, has potential for conflict.

A particular incident, that of a commonplace eviction and its aftermath, serves to give a taste of the general problem. Five bailiffs from the City Housing Department come to repossess a terraced house from a group of Dreadlock squatters. An Inspector and several policemen stand by against a breach of the peace. The group evicted comprises ten boys and a pregnant girl. As bailiffs tin up the windows, they gather on the pavement, protesting. The leader is the sharply – but now shabbily – dressed lad who had come to the station four days previously to claim Paul Anthony, the young lad involved in the wheel theft. The lad himself, escaped once again from 'care', stands silently by, worn trousers reaching to his calves, wide-eyed and lost as ever.

They are joined by the thin scarfaced youth from the squat in Blank Road. He stands on the steps outside the locked front door, his arms spread wide. What will become of them, he demands to know, where will they go? The leader becomes even more agitated. He jumps on to the low wall in front of the house, shouting, waving his arms. 'I leave ten pound on the carpet upstairs, right. It gone, man. It arl t'ief. This lot,' pointing to the bailiffs now preparing to leave, 'take arl we money. And you police, you do fuck arl. What arl you doing, tell me that? What arl you doing bout me ten pound?' As he speaks, his gestures grow wilder. Resentment takes possession of him. He mouths accusations and obscenities in a high pitched yell. 'No use shouting like that,' the Inspector says. 'If you have a complaint to make, just come down here and make it quietly.' The youth rants on for five minutes or more. A few neighbours come out and join the small group of police on the pavement. They all stare at the youth blankly. '. . . Fucking bastards. Is arl you do, fuck arl . . .' he screams. 'All right, come down then, and give me the details,' says the Inspector.

The youth finally gets off the wall. 'All right, we talk here then, right, where there's a captive audience,' he says. He claims he had left two £5 notes on a carpet which was rolled up by bailiffs and thrown from a first storey window. 'But have you looked around for the money?' the Inspector asks. The youth's information is confused and inconsistent. The Inspector's face shows his doubts. 'I'll make enquiries,' he says. 'And since there's no address now to contact you at, I suggest you come to Thornhill Road Station in a few days' time.'

The scarfaced lad and others then complain that a cassette recorder has been taken from the house by the police. 'I'm checking on it as suspected stolen property,' says the Inspector. A chorus of abuse follows. 'What you take it for? Just because we black, right . . . We ain't t'ief, man. Is arl you lot, fucking police bastards. . . . We, arl we look for is peace . . . We is men of peace, man.'

More protests follow about the eviction itself. What will they all do for a place to live? The Inspector and I explain (he for the second time) that the police have nothing to do with the eviction. That is a matter for the Housing Department. The police job is to stand by, keep the peace. The group calms down, questions us about housing and asks me to meet them that afternoon at the Area Housing Department.

One of the youths and the pregnant girl are the first to be interviewed there. 'Only God can help us,' he says. She gives her name to a woman housing official, tells her that she is six months' pregnant, and that the youth lives with her. 'And what's your name?' asks the housing official. 'Bogle.' 'How do you spell it?' 'You tell her,' says Bogle to his girl. 'I ain't telling her how to spell the name,' the girl replies. 'B-O-G-L-E,' I say. It's a common Jamaican name. 'You don't want to tell her,' Bogle says, 'She has the job here. She should know how to spell.'

The housing official explains that there are many demands on local council accommodation, and few places available. Only the girl can therefore be offered a place to live, which will be in a hostel until more permanent accommodation becomes available. 'Why can't the boys have a house too?' asks the girl. 'Many people are in need in the area,' says the housing official. 'Accommodation must be allocated according to priority of need. For the boys, there is nothing now.'

After the interview I explain matters to the group as a whole. 'All right. But what about the ten pound? . . . The police, they the biggest thieves of all.' 'Do you really believe that?' 'I don't believe it. I know it,' says Bogle. Back in the station at Thornhill Road I check on the scarfaced 'man of peace' to find he has three convictions for muggings as well as others for affray and for assaulting a police officer. The cassette recorder taken from the squat is later found to be property stolen from a youth movement day centre (providing mainly for young West Indians) following a break-in two months previously. Enquiries bring no information about the two £5 notes alleged as stolen from the squat. Did they ever exist? In such a context, realities and solutions seem equally hard to discern.

Issues of police liaison

What is apparent in the Handsworth context is the extent to which police functions relate to those of other statutory and voluntary services. All confront faces of what are, in essence, common problems. And the nature of those problems make it clear that no service can work effectively in isolation, nor through purely reactive policies. The sub-divisional commander, Superintendent Webb, therefore wisely puts primary emphasis on linking police tasks with those of other agencies and upon activating community backing and preventive resources. In such ways he seeks to create a climate of collaboration and trust for his men to work in.

Superintendent Webb gives an admirable lead in creating and developing liaison with a wide range of local organisations. Personal links play a great part here, liaison between police and social services, in particular, owing much to the understanding and constant contacts between Superintendent Webb and the Area Manager for Social Services, Mike Townsend. Relationships between police and community relations organisations are also improving. A Police Liaison Committee set up in 1976 meets monthly to discuss police–community problems, and a scheme is to be put into effect whereby certain approved community volunteers are available for advice in cases of difficulty or dispute following arrests.

Yet Handsworth remains something of a minefield for liaison, especially amongst West Indian groups. Here the inheritance of the Caribbean plantation culture comes home: a lack of strong family and community structures and values; tensions and divisions of colour and class reinforcing each other; traditions of anarchic individualism fragmenting purposes, organisation and leadership. To these may be added the conflicts and insularities particular to Jamaican society, from which – as also at Brixton – more than half Handsworth's West Indians come.

Characteristically, 'leaders' abound, some self-proclaimed, though there are few signs of collective approaches to community policy and action. The leadership scene is riven by ideological differences and personal distrust; and motives appear equally mixed. Some leaders make useful and effective efforts to develop their community's capacity for self-help and advancement. Others seem more intent to feed – and thereby feed on – local feelings of social/racial disadvantage and anti-social, even criminal, attitudes. Integrity and opportunism mingle freely here; and difficulties of distinguishing which from which are complicated at times as media of mass communication, seemingly intent on instant issues, give certain leaders either false prominence or illusory status as representative community voices. In reality, few 'leaders' command widespread support as yet; and alarmingly few West Indian groups in Handsworth have either major community significance or a developed capacity for effective community action. The local Asian communities provide a vital point of contrast in this respect, and the increasing disparity between the rates of advancement of Asian and West Indian communities locally and nationally owes much to the comparative strength of Asian family and communal structures, traditions and values. In Handsworth, as Asian shopkeepers complain to the police of being menaced by West Indian youths, fears already grow that from this disparity of achievement will breed resentment and conflict.

In terms of numbers, the most substantial West Indian organisation in Handsworth is the Faith and Confidence[4] Fellowship Social Club, providing leisure facilities and activities for some 500 members. Its clientele consists mainly of first generation immigrants, now well settled in the area, who like to drink and play cards or dominoes together. In the evenings round the domino tables the atmosphere is vivid and intense: men of varying shapes and hues, rolypoly black to wrinkled brown, in headgear varying from old school caps to straw boaters, laughing, shouting in triumph, slamming down dominoes with dramatic gusto. And whilst such men express general concern about the predicaments of West Indian youth in Handsworth, and the need for youth opportunities and facilities to be improved in the area, there is only resentment against the Dreadlock delinquents who bring shame to their people. As for accusation of police harassment: 'Harassment, they don't know what the word mean. If any of the boys go back to their own country, then they really find out. Then they go suffer harassment. If the policemen there say "Keep moving", then he keep moving. If he don't move, bam, bam, bam. Then he keep moving . . .'

Similar sentiments may be heard from West Indians in the handful of local pubs with West Indian licensees.*

> 'These youth, they don't want to work. They're unemployables . . . And they no more Rasta than fly. True Rastas are good, quiet people. These lads is hooligans, man, just hooligans. A disgrace to us all. They should have taken a shipload of them to mid-Atlantic, just sink them all there.'

In certain clubs, feelings run stronger, especially against the youth who hang around on the 'front line' (the junction of Soho and Villa Roads). 'When the weather is warm, they all out there like the birds sitting on the trees.' The image is that of the John Crows – the turkey vultures – sat in a line on a tree in Jamaica, waiting for carrion. West Indians running clubs claim that these youths discourage customers by their threatening behaviour, and are ruining trade. They press the police for stronger action to clear the youths from the streets. Superintendent Webb points out that he cannot use the police in a repressive role, nor can police take action unless the youths commit a criminal act or a breach of the peace, or unless specific complaints are brought against them by mem-

---

* Though West Indians now run several pubs in the area, there is minimal evidence of their going into trades. The point of contrast is again supplied by local Asians, whose shops multiply, particularly down the Soho Road.

bers of the public. But it is apparent that those who privately press for stronger action against the youths on the front line hold back from any public stance for fear both of being branded as traitors to their own kind, and of physical retribution. (One club owner's car has already been slashed and smashed up by Dreadlocks.)

For the police, the situation is not without irony. On the one hand they are denounced for harassing West Indian youth; on the other they are pressed – by West Indians – to take stronger action against West Indian youth. And police problems of identifying representative community viewpoints do not end there, for even within a single small community group or organisation very disparate voices may be heard.

Such ambiguities currently surround the work of Harambee, generally regarded as the most effective of local West Indian self-help organisations. At the time of writing, Harambee houses some 12 homeless children (nine boys and three girls), and hopes to increase that number to 18 by the end of 1977, thanks to the provision of a new building financed by Urban Aid. One-fourth of the cost of the project is met by the City Social Services Department, and provision is made for joint supervision of the boys and girls by social workers and Harambee wardens. Harambee also runs a multi-racial nursery for 31 children; provides English and Maths classes, each twice a week, and offers a yearly four-week summer school in black cultural studies, attended by some 400 young people.

Since the influence of black cultural studies is widespread, the matter and manner of its teaching is of critical local concern; and ambiguities abound here, deriving from disparate ideologies and disparate interpretations of young people's needs. Should emphases fall upon the history and achievement of the Negro race or upon the bitter injustice and exploitation they have suffered? Should the main aim be to create a sense of identity and purpose of being amongst young blacks or to breed resentment of and alienation from white racist society? Should young people be guided towards the understanding and skills needed to make out in this society or incited to resist and reject the oppressive system of Babylon? The harsh realities of Handsworth and Britain here and now, or the improbable dream of Ethiopia and Africa, there and then: where should the focus be?

Beyond such questions are the wider issues. To what extent do concepts of 'culture' in 'black' or 'race' terms have validity or reality? Can 'culture' be conceived or comprehended in terms other than those of particular societies in specific locales? And in the foreground are the problems evoked by differing approaches to teaching. 'Too often the teaching is emotional and destructive rather than objective and constructive,' comments the Chairman of Harambee, Dennis Nelson. And he recognises the weight of responsibility that teachers of black cultural studies must accept, and the gravity of that work's implications for local youth and society.

From the differing emphases derive differing views both of the delinquent sub-culture and of the police. From the determinist angle of vision, the Dreadlocks are seen essentially as infected victims of a society that has condemned them to educational, social, racial and economic disadvantage, and whose injustices and tyranny drive them inevitably – and thus to some extent legitimately – to violence against that society. Other community workers see the Dreads rather as sources of infection, dominating, indoctrinating and criminalising other West Indian youth, and thereby endangering the health and reputation of the West Indian community as a whole. By the same yardsticks, police may be seen either as the repressive arm of Babylon, with whom no truck is possible, or as legitimate partners in containing social infection.

The complexities do not end there, however. There is also considerable disparity between what is preached and what is practised by leading protagonists in this sphere. Some in public loose a flood of militant rhetoric and polemic, thus maintaining credibility amongst their followers (demagogues, like preachers, are primary figures on the Caribbean scene), yet in private show a willingness for interchange and compromise with Babylon that could well, if known, shake the faith of followers. Because of such political, or politic, discrepancies between public utterances and private acts, polarisations of local attitudes are often rather less than they seem to be, or as they are commonly interpreted.

Whilst talking with a leader of a West Indian self-help club at the end of May, all such ambiguities came into play. His starting point was the futility of even discussing co-operation with police who were simply agents of a capitalist society whose racism had infected and enslaved the whole Caribbean. Slowly it emerged that Superintendent Webb had come to visit him several times to discuss arrangements for African Liberation Day celebrations in Handsworth Park. 'But it's a waste of time. Even if *he* has good intentions, he can't do anything. It's impossible because of the racialism in all coppers.' He went on to assert that National Front influence was now growing fast within the police service. Yet it soon became clear that understandings had been reached about the conduct of the celebrations, including a 'low profile' police presence. The leader doubted if he could believe this, however, alleging that another policeman had told him otherwise. 'But if it's possible to talk with the police on this issue, isn't it possible to negotiate on other issues?' At this, he withdrew to his opening position: the impossibility of communication with capitalist racialist society.

In the event, African Liberation Day celebrations extended over three days, 4–6 June 1977. They attracted West Indians from all over the country, with cultural events during the first two days preceding a march of some 600 people on the final day, banners flying and drums sounding, to three hours of music and spectacle in Handsworth Park. Anti-police pamphlets and 'Flame' were distributed to the crowd, proclaiming that 'The Police are out for blood. We cannot sit down and take it any more.' No incidents or arrests involving police were reported during the whole period of the celebrations, and on the following day, organisers took it upon themselves to clear the park of litter.

Understanding, negotiation and co-operation between West Indians and police were thereby shown to be both desired and possible in Handsworth. On the one hand, the police demonstrate a growing willingness and capacity for interchange and collaboration. On the other hand, the severity of the problems posed by growing numbers of disadvantaged West Indian youth, with their consequences of crime and violence, draws – or impels – more and more local leaders towards the middle ground where at least a climate for co-operation, if not some measure of consensus, becomes attainable. Example: a brother of the Rastafarian Church willing to help the police draw distinctions between the true adherents of the faith and the criminalised sub-culture; and to help the youths associating with the faith towards clearer understanding of police responsibilities and functions.

Given the deep divisions of Handsworth, however – human, social, economic, cultural, religious, political and racial – and its guttering physical condition, the path for mediation remains bitter and wearisome. Even the most guarded optimism is something of a luxury here.

4   *Preventive strategies*

Most of those with whom I spoke in Handsworth agree – implicitly or explicitly – that problems of police/West Indian relationships demand strategies both of more effective control and of more effective care, directed primarily at youth at risk; and that such strategies must run together.

One component of these strategies relates to police policies and operations. Here a first priority is to augment police strength. To argue a special case for C1 sub-division would raise a host of dissenting hands, though I believe there is as much a case for designating areas of special police concern, including Handsworth, on a national scale as there is for identifying areas of national economic concern. Yet it is certainly reasonable to suggest that the sub-divisional uniform strength (20 per cent below establishment) should be brought up to the average of the West Midlands force as a whole (10 per cent below establishment). This would give the sub-division some twenty more – and preferably more experienced – officers, permitting additional police strength to be deployed in the area of special concern (see page 7).

A second priority is to provide more effective and more locally responsive police coverage of the critical areas, with emphasis shifting from car to foot patrolling. This could be furthered by reallocating the area covered by present beats 6, 7, 8, 9, 10 and parts of 5 and 17 into nine smaller beats, with a permanent beat officer on each, and by providing stimulus for greater co-ordination between the work of the PBOs and that of the other arms of the service.

If certain uniform unit and CID officers were to be given specific responsibilities within the critical area, for example, this might make for closer liaison with PBOs as well as for close contact with the community. And liaison would be reinforced if, or their side, PBOs gave greater priority to handling local incidents and to channelling flows of information to CID and other specialist units. Relationships might be further eased if more suitably experienced young officers were encouraged to take on beat functions, thus reducing distinctions and divisions between the various arms of the service. In such ways, a further police priority would be served: to bring about more effective integration of functions.

Such integration could well make both for increased efficiency and for better morale, particularly amongst the PBOs, who would then be able to realise their own role as an essential component of mainstream police functions. And by reducing the dangers of various arms of the service presenting differing, if not contrasting and confusing faces to the public (now soft now hard, now friendly now aggressive), it could also serve to create greater and more sustained trust in the police amongst the community.

But the primary object of creating more locally based, more locally responsive police systems is to raise the quality of contact policing. The experience of Handsworth shows this to be the crucial issue in any discussions of police functions and relationships. Yet here, as elsewhere, it appears to have too low a priority and status; and this undervaluation will continue whilst the reactive role of the police continues to take commanding precedence over the preventive role. Given the intense pressures of local circumstances, this imbalance between the two roles is, in the short term, understandable. Yet in the long term, over-emphasis on the reactive role can only lead the police into paths of greater isolation from the public; into more distrustful perspectives upon the community, whereby it may come to be viewed in the image of its malefactors rather than in the round; into growing risks of a 'siege' mentality, making misunderstanding, conflict and confrontation ever more possible; and into attempting to sustain a fire-brigade role under ever-increasing pressures, until demands inevitably outstretch resources. In brief, the consequences of reactive policies are finally unacceptable in human, professional and economic terms.

The fundamental police priority is therefore that of bringing the reactive and preventive roles into a balance appropriate to long-term objectives; and in Handsworth Superintendent Webb's initiatives already demonstrate how professionally vital is the role which aims to mobilise community support and preventive resources. (It is a role that will prove ever more essential for all statutory social services in our society, for human and economic as well as for professional reasons.) Difficulties attend that role within the police service as amongst the public. On both sides are suspicion of, and resistance to, police-community initiatives.

'Our business is to feel collars', some police say. 'Why waste time on talk, especially with some of those buggers who do nothing but knock us.' Yet even in these blinkered terms, the community role is justified, for a climate of liaison and co-operation certainly enables police both to feel *more* collars and to be more certain that they are feeling the *right* collars.

As Handsworth demonstrates, the more tense and disturbed the area, the more brutally apparent it is that policing is not a matter for police alone, and that the task of alerting and aiding the community towards self-regulation is a mainstream police function. For Superintendent Webb it is an operational command function. He therefore spends much of his time out on the ground, looking to create networks of liaison and collaboration, and ready to respond to – or anticipate – the conflicts and crises that can spring so quick on these troubled streets.

The roots of preventive resources are the structures, relationships and values of society, the inherent and essential forces of care and control – or to put it more pertinently, the essential *police* forces. It follows that a primary task of a police service is that of realising or activating those police forces in society. In Handsworth such a prescription raises thorny issues. Family and community structures, relationships and values are strong only amongst Asian groups, notably those least influenced by and 'integrated' with British ways of life. And whilst there is extensive evidence of 'communities' in terms of group cultures and relationships, there is sparse evidence of 'community' between groups or on an area basis, other than a community of interest in guarding property and living in peace.

Problems of norms are central here; and in Handsworth the norm-confusion which characterises declining urban areas within the flux of contemporary industrial society is multiplied by the norm-disparity which characterises areas of multicultural occupation. Local police are therefore unable to make those assumptions of a reasonable identity of purpose and values between themselves and local society which, in effect, secure a base for appropriate decisions and confident action.

The task of activating the inherent self-regulatory forces in society is thus a good deal more complex in Handsworth than in areas of greater norm stability. So that it is all the more imperative to have men of high quality on the ground here capable of enacting this front-line police function: experienced and committed officers able to generate trust, to create sustained relationships, to stimulate activities, to be aware of connections between the preventive roles of the police service and those of other statutory and voluntary agencies, and to contribute to collaborative projects within the local society.

Such qualities and skills demand special training programmes, oriented where possible – as this study is – around 'on the ground' case studies. Experience-based approaches to training, making extensive use of local police and community resources of knowledge and experience, enable officers to view and analyse their functions and problems within real perspectives, and to realise live connections between their functions and those of other agencies. And by the very concentration and complexity of its problems, Handsworth affords admirable opportunities not only for local training of this kind, but also for the training of those who, at regional and national levels, wish to explore more deeply, through the experience of a key area of urban industrial society, the implications of contemporary social and race problems for police policies and operations. Such studies are still too often confined to the classroom in police education at all levels.

Given appropriate priorities and training, the preventive influence and capability of the police might be greatly extended, both among general community groups, such as the residents' associations, offering vital multi-ethnic bases for community self-regulation, and amongst West Indian groups having authority and links amongst the youth most at risk.

And as beat officers, in particular, become more effective as reference points for area attitudes and policies, so does their capacity to help – and even train – local people to be more active in self-regulation, whether in controlling crowds at local events or in guarding their area against vandalism. The special constabulary might also be given a more specific community role in support of local beat constables, though its rank structure and inappropriate training at present bar it from effective integration with core police functions.

The ideal here – that of the policeman as the focus of a self-regulating community – closely resembles the original conception of the office of constable, the practical objectives being the prevention and control of many of those minor delinquencies and disorders which now usurp so much of the time and energies of the police in their reactive role. In this perspective, preventive policing becomes an increasingly fundamental component of mainstream policies and operations.

Prevention strategies are most effective where local resources of care and control – those of the community and those of statutory and voluntary agencies – are most fully mobilised within a framework of concerted policy. In Handsworth, as in the society as a whole, there is scant evidence of such a framework, despite useful interchange and collaboration developing between both policy-makers and 'ground' practitioners in certain agencies. Yet the problems of local youth at risk, in particular, demand nothing less than a co-ordinated response from those statutory and voluntary agencies whose work bears on those problems. Failing concerted policy and action, more and more youth will inevitably drift into the already established patterns of alienation and delinquency, thus reinforcing what has become, in effect, a local culture of disaffection, with alarming consequences in terms of increased pressures on the resources of individual agencies as well as in human terms within the community, especially for the old and the defenceless, those who will suffer most from that culture.

One immediate local need is therefore to set up a forum for inter-agency dialogue and policy specifically relating to youth problems in Handsworth. There is room for an initiative under independent sponsorship which creates opportunities for interchange between those bodies to whom the problem gives concern – police, employers, trade unions, social services, probation and youth services, education, careers and employment services, the magistracy, the Churches (including branches of the Rastafarian faith) and residents' associations, together with West Indian and Asian self-help, community, social and religious groups.

Such interchange could usefully be directed towards specific objectives – firstly, the ways in which the various agencies can co-operate in the practical tasks of controlling youth delinquency and crime; secondly, the ways in which they can collaborate to offer creative alternatives to youth at risk from idleness, disaffection and criminality through improved employment, work experience,* training, educational, cultural, and social opportunities; thirdly, the ways in which they can create amongst themselves more permanent networks of liaison directed towards those ends.

Questions of how to provide better work experience, education and training opportunities, particularly for the vital 14–19 age group – those too young to be served by Handsworth's new, handsome and costly Skillcentre† – would certainly have a central place in such discussions. Occupational Selection courses, Short Industrial courses and a Job Creation programme are currently (1977) provided at Selly Oak and Perry Barr by the City of Birmingham Careers Service, but local work experience and training facilities for the younger age group are limited, not least because industrial investment in the area is low. There is a crucial need for 'bridging' programmes preparing those who leave school – often before age 16 – with poor educational attainments to go on to make use of established further education and training courses. Some of these programmes could usefully be organised through, or in collaboration with, community self-help groups, who have already established credibility and influence amongst youth of West Indian origin or descent; though in taking on such work, these groups would almost certainly require support from statutory sources, for few, if any, currently possess the management, training and supervisory skills to mount such programmes from their own resources.

A further main theme would be that of providing better cultural, social and recreational facilities for youth at risk. The provision of club facilities is already under local discussion,

---

* Sentencing policy could also have an important role here through the use of community service orders.

† The Holyhead Road Skillcentre cost some £5–6 million to set up, approximately £1 million a year to maintain. Currently it provides practical training for some 200 students aged 19 and over, its target student number being 550.

though opinions seem divided both as to the nature and the management of such provision. The ideal, perhaps, is that of a club in a convenient central area offering education and training as well as cultural, social and recreational facilities. Yet such a project is likely to prove lengthy and costly. If it were to be approved, conditions would need to be laid down to ensure that those who wish to use it contribute to its making, and that its facilities are guaranteed against dangers of usurpation by dominant groups.

The success of such a club would depend upon the quality of activities generated by those who use it; and more fundamentally, upon its capacity to reach out to, and provide for, the youth at risk. In meeting the first of these objectives, the police could well play a valuable role by providing voluntary trade and recreational skills. They are also well placed to co-operate with the Social Services and other agencies in a programme of camps and other outings for local youth. A pilot scheme for a camp in North Wales is already planned by the Public Liaison Department of the West Midlands Police, and this could provide a lead for further schemes on an inter-agency basis, involving both statutory and voluntary organisations.

To meet the second objective, activities in a central club would almost certainly need to be reinforced by work on detachment in the squats where the youth most at risk congregate – a daunting task even for suitably skilled and experienced West Indians who command some measure of credibility amongst the Dreadlocks.

Are such suggestions merely pious in a scene so highly charged with potential for conflict? I think not. My impressions are that the forces of moderation are a good deal stronger than vociferous extremist voices proclaim; that the 'silent majority' of local people seek above all peace, order and security based on the rule of law; that as violence mounts, more and more 'leaders' stand ready to take paths of mediation; and that even amongst the youth most at risk, there is a desperate thirst for learning, understanding, skills, creative relationships.

What can be achieved by collaborative policies and action

on a local scale is limited, of course, by the nature and quality of political and economic decisions taken at municipal, regional and national levels about industrial investment, housing policy, educational provision, urban renewal, etc. Yet communal analyses of local needs can prove useful as sources of advice and influence even for decisions at those levels, as well as providing vital bases for local self-regulation and self-help.

And collaborative projects at local level are helpful in terms not only of opportunities and facilities but also of community relations. The spectacle of police and West Indian organisations acting in useful concert, for example, could do much to activate West Indian support for and co-operation with the police, both amongst groups and individuals; and to engender greater trust and confidence in West Indians amongst the police. In brief, it could help bring relationships between police and West Indians into line with those between police and natives of Handsworth.

5   Issues for discussion and research

Yet whatever improvements come about in police–West Indian relationships in Handsworth, local problems in this sphere will continue to centre on the youth at risk. And the underlying questions here are of national and international as well as of local concern. Are the central issues those of race or colour? Or do they more closely relate to the cultural inheritance of the transplant colonial society in the Caribbean? Or to the distinctive contradictions and conflicts of Jamaican society? Or rather to the nature of the urban environment in which they are growing up, characterised by housing decay, high unemployment and an insular culture? Or are they simply variants of issues relating to youth as a whole in contemporary society? Or – as seems much more likely to me – do the problems of young West Indians in Handsworth involve a complex of factors, those mentioned above amongst them, generated from an interaction of social/cultural factors deriving from West Indian society and social/economic factors deriving from their immediate city environment?

If this is so, it points the need for further analysis of issues discussed here within comparative frames of reference, aimed at defining both the causal factors and relationships between those factors. In particular, we need to know:

1. In what ways and for what reasons do problems for police and society associated with West Indian youth in Handsworth resemble, and differ from, similar problems associated with West Indian youth in other areas?
    Comparative studies could usefully be developed here:
    (a) between social and police problems in Handsworth and those in another major area of West Indian settlement (e.g. Brixton);
    (b) between problems of Antillean youth settlement in Britain (e.g. Handsworth and Brixton) and those in Holland (e.g. parts of Amsterdam);
    (c) between West Indian youth problems in areas (i) with high and low densities of West Indian population (e.g. Brixton and Slough); (ii) of greater and less social/ economic disadvantage (e.g. Handsworth and Bedford);
    (d) between the problems of youth from different island backgrounds in areas of West Indian settlement;
    (e) between the social and police problems of West Indian-born and British-born youth of West Indian stock in areas of West Indian settlement.
2. In what ways and for what reasons do the social and police

problems associated with young West Indians resemble, and differ from, those associated with British and Asian youth?

Comparative studies on these issues might be made:

(a) between the social problems and patterns of criminality of West Indian and Asian youth in Handsworth;

(b) between the social problems and patterns of criminality of West Indian and British youth in disadvantaged areas of Birmingham;

(c) between evidence of crime, violence and alienation amongst West Indian youth in Handsworth and that amongst native youth in, say, Kirkby New Town and parts of Glasgow.

3. What background factors are significant amongst West Indian offenders aged between 12 and 20, e.g. place of birth; island stock; family history and relationships; educational history and attainment; employment record; peer group associations; previous crime record?

Issues of police–West Indian relationships in Handsworth also point towards three other related areas of study:

1. Of police policies, attitudes, staffing and recruitment, organisational structures and training in areas of contrasting social, cultural and economic circumstances and norms, and of the ways these factors relate to the quality of contact policing and to the qualities of relationships between police and society.

2. Of allegations of police violence against West Indian youth.

3. Of the effects of crimes of violence against persons and personal property on those who are the victims of such crimes.

I suggest that studies on these lines could provide society with far firmer bases than it now has both for disentangling myths from realities in the troubled and emotive sphere under discussion and for devising appropriate remedial policies. For despite the fact that much contemporary discussion of the issues involved tends to stress particular race relations or political aspects, the issues themselves remain complex. In this sense, there are no blacks and whites in Handsworth. It is all shades of grey.

Part II
Handsworth
Revisited

6 *Perspectives*

If only one could begin by setting out 'the facts' of policing in Handsworth. But of course there are no 'facts' of absolute authority: only a mass of evidence, quantitative and qualitative, of greater or less validity, none of it amenable to precise measurement; and in addition, a plethora of diverse perspectives. And since perceptions of insecurity, personal and collective, are so central to valuations of policing in Handsworth, I make no apology for starting from the evidence of the senses.

The Brown test is to walk local streets after the pubs turn out at nights, to see how I and others feel at that time. Are our mouths dry? Do our feet quicken? Are our senses at ease or on tenterhooks?

Gradually, over the last four years, the fears and tensions of 1977 have seemed, in some measure, to recede, in particular because of a growing passage of people about their business on local streets at this and most other hours of night and day. Are they about because there is less street crime? Is there in fact less street crime, or are there merely perceptions of less street crime? And has either the one or the other come about because more people are out and about? Whatever the nature of the interactions here, many main streets, at least, are all buzz and bustle as never before.

And the contrasts of Handsworth seem even more vivid. As before, black, brown and white kids play in littered, derelict streets not far from where Canada geese strut head in air over green, pleasant and very select golf links. But now the contrasts jostle each other almost everywhere. Demolition sites confronting lines of repointed, repainted façades. Decaying houses, windows and doors tinned up, junk and detritus strewn over front areas, cheek by jowl with impeccable properties, immaculate lawns. Rusty bangers parked bumper to bumper with newly registered Mercedes saloons. Elegant ladies in bright saris, hovering over fruit stalls like birds of paradise, almost rubbing shoulders with black boys in woolly hats, rubbed jeans, worn gym shoes.

Handsworth is perceptibly changing. Evidence abounds. And whilst ideologues paint pictures of Handsworth as an increasingly deprived and segregated area, local streets and public places already suggest a more complex story. This is expressed not only in visual terms – ranging from renovated properties and their new brick walls in some of the side streets to the brand new sports centre that now surveys well-kept pitches, neat flower-beds, children on swings, old men on bowling greens in the local park – but also, and perhaps more pertinently, in a growing sense of dynamic amongst the movements and purposes of local people.

Who cannot feel this sense of dynamic now on the main thoroughfare, the Soho Road? Stand still there a moment at midday, amongst the blacks, whites and browns thronging the shops and stalls, mingling freely and at ease amongst the fresh fruit, vegetable and curry smells, and the vans and cars unloading their goods at the kerbside. And between snarls of traffic, listen to the ring of cash registers. Count the number of Mercedes passing per minute. Survey the range of goods and services on display. Then go and poke your nose in the storehouses and workshops, where more and more pens mark more and more ledgers; where more and more hands feed more and more sewing machines; where business thrives and profits multiply.

Here Asian businesses seem to have spread like wildfire over the past four years, as a new nation of shopkeepers moves in, one that is ready to work from dawn to dusk and beyond. More than three-quarters of all shops on the Soho Road – where property prices soar – are already (mid-1981) in Asian hands, no more than a handful of West Indian businesses dotted amongst them.

Business goes on into the night; and after dark, the clubs on the 'front line' near the junction of Soho and Villa Roads begin to seethe once more with people. Clothes seem sharper, rhythms more insistent, parked cars bigger and better than before. So that, all in all, Handsworth now inceasingly appears as a place to come to rather than to go from: in no sense a place apart.

But to what extent does the evidence of the senses relate to the statistical evidence? As usual, overall crime statistics tell us precious little, either in absolute or comparative terms. And even in depicting trends, they can readily mislead. Thus at first sight the increase in reported crime on the C1 (Handsworth) police sub-division over the four years from the beginning of 1977 to the end of 1980 looks modest – 8 per cent, against a West Midlands Force increase of 7.7 per cent. Yet both 1978 and 1979 saw substantial decreases over 1977 totals, whilst 1980 witnessed a 17.7 per cent increase over 1979 (from 6,073 to 7,137) against a Force increase of 12.5 per cent over the same period. This trend continued into early 1981, though very unevenly, as often happens in winter and early spring, when chance factors such as the vagaries of the 'sodden and unkind' weather in the English Midlands tend to count heavily, cold and wet being major factors in crime control.

Handsworth Sub-Division
Reported Crime Summary: 1 January 1977 – 31 June 1981

	1977	1978	1979	1980	1981
January	468	522	398	452	702
February	423	453	351	580	552
March	528	475	428	595	710
April	549	486	536	630	667
May	541	520	510	614	704
June	529	540	602	585	717
July	630	524	556	628	
August	646	492	614	650	
September	557	525	552	573	
October	584	552	509	617	
November	597	437	513	599	
December	554	401	504	614	
TOTAL	6606	5927	6073	7137	

Yet whilst trends in overall reported crime on the sub-division are rising, trends in reported cases of robbery and theft from the person – the street crime which has been a, if not the, major cause of public insecurity in Handsworth – offer slight crumbs of hope. During 1977, 322 cases had been reported (an average of 27 per month), 222 in the second half of the year. The peak came in January 1978, with 47 cases reported. Then came an abrupt drop to 14 in the following month, and from February until the end of 1978, reported cases averaged only 16 per month, the yearly total being 220. This level was maintained throughout 1979 (218 cases, averaging 18 per month), and during the first half to 1980; but in the second half of the year, reported cases again began to rise, peaking to 35 in December. In all, 253 cases were reported in 1980 (an average of 21 per month); and this represented a sub-divisional decrease of 14.29 per cent against a Force increase of 10.31 per cent for this category of crime over the four-year period.

The statistical evidence is thus in line with, and reinforces, the perceptions of many local people – a sense of gradually diminishing insecurity on their own streets. Caution is the watchword here, however. During the first five months of 1981, reported cases of robbery/theft from the person on the sub-division totalled 116 (65 robberies; 51 thefts from the person), an average of 23 per month, representing a significant rise (24.73 per cent) over the comparable period in 1980. And the great predominance of youths and young men of West Indian origin in these categories of crime continues to be a major cause of concern.

The origins of assailants were identified in 55 of the 65 cases of robbery, 49 (89.1 per cent) of them allegedly involving ninety-one assailants of West Indian origin, and 6 allegedly involving thirteen white assailants. The origins of assailants were also identified in 37 of the 51 cases of theft from the person, 33 (89.2 per cent) of them allegedly involving forty assailants of West Indian origin, and 4 allegedly involving five whites. West Indian involvement in these crime categories thus continues at 1977 levels, Asian involvement remaining at zero level.

The quality as well as the quantity of crime of this kind is also of prime concern. In 1981, attacks on women and the elderly are still commonplace, some accompanied by frightening violence, e.g. to two elderly shopkeepers, each of whom needed some 150 stitches to their headwounds; and to an 84-year-old woman ex-teacher, whose face was savagely and bloodily battered with a milk bottle, and who at the time of writing (mid-1981) remains in hospital. (By contrast, three of the four murders in the area in recent years have been Indian, one British and none West Indian.)

Similar ambiguities surround the categories of sub-divisional street crime covering motor vehicle offences:

	1977	1978	1979	1980
Theft of motor vehicles	1173	819	777	909
Unlawful taking of motor vehicles	227	157	177	176
Theft from motor vehicles	443	421	431	545

As with street robbery and theft, reported cases of theft of motor vehicles fell significantly in early 1978 – from 102 in January to 86 in February – and both thefts and unlawful taking of motor vehicles continued to decrease during 1978 and 1979, thefts from motor vehicles remaining fairly constant. The number of reported cases in all three categories rose again during 1980, though over the four-year period under review, thefts and unlawful taking of motor vehicles reported on the sub-division fell by 23.59 per cent against a Force decrease of 9.25 per cent. In contrast, reported cases of sub-divisional thefts from motor vehicles rose by 23.02 per cent over the four-year period against a Force increase of 18.51 per cent. Detectives dealing with these cases note with concern the still small but significantly growing number of young Asians responsible for thefts of motor vehicles, and contrast their purposeful commercial motives with the often haphazard 'joy-riding' motives of young West Indians: 'There's very little organised crime in Handsworth. But what there is, is down to Indians. Mostly lads, 17, 18, 19, who've lost their culture. No more than Brummagem ragtags, really . . .'

Whilst street crime reported on the sub-division decreased over the four-year period, both in absolute and in comparative terms, reported break-in offences substantially increased over the same period:

	1977	1978	1979	1980
Burglary from dwelling houses	1119	1074	1459	1709
Burglary from other buildings	1034	1007	1047	1170
TOTAL	2153	2081	2506	2879

These statistics represent a sub-divisional increase in reported cases of burglary from dwelling houses of 52.73 per cent over the four-year period, against a Force increase of 36.36 per cent. Reported burglary from other buildings on the sub-division, however, remained fairly constant until 1980, when they rose again to make up a 13.15 per cent increase over the four-year period. Favoured targets at the time of writing are stack stereo and video cassette units, each valued around £500, the latter increasingly commonplace in local households for showing Indian films to Punjabi-speaking family groups. But since clear-up rates for offences of this kind are admittedly 'dismal', valid generalisations cannot be made about the origins of offenders.

Burglaries from dwelling houses continued to grow rapidly in Handsworth during 1981 – to the extent that 240 cases were reported in October 1981 against a monthly average of 142 in 1980 – and this growth has been accompanied by increasing evidence that groups of young West Indians are being commissioned for burglary to steal video-cassette units. For the offenders, the added attractions of this category of crime – apart, of course, from the very low detection rates – are that it currently evokes far less public outcry than street robbery and commands far lighter sentences – often non-custodial – in the courts.

Continual observation and the evidence of local people also suggests that crime is a good deal more widespread in Handsworth than the statistics indicate. Petty theft from shops by young West Indians is of particular concern, especially when accompanied by abuse and hustling of the (mainly) ageing whites of the area. The reluctance of Asians – especially Asian women – to report crime may also be a telling factor in masking its true incidence and impact. Overall, however, the local patterns indicated by the statistics – of less crime on the street, more crime off the street – seem reasonably valid.

When seeking to identify factors which have shaped these changes in local crime patterns over the last four years, evidence offers itself from several different perspectives. Especially tempting is the apparent connection between the drafting into Handsworth of additional police manpower for local 'contact' policing in January 1978, together with the greater priority and purpose given to the work of the Permanent Beat Officers at that time, and the radical decrease in various categories of street crime (robbery; theft from the person; theft of motor vehicles) reported in the following month. But that's just too good to be true. I do not doubt the long-term preventive and deterrent value of PBO work on the sub-division, and of the networks of understanding and cooperation these officers are creating in the area, but the very nature of their work virtually precludes dramatic short term effects. So that here greater weight must be given to the 'law-enforcement' perspective, which correlates the rapid drop in street crime with the arrest and subsequent imprisonment of some half dozen hard-core offenders of West Indian origin who also acted as local ringleaders and motivators of crimes of this kind.

A number of other offences had been committed whilst they were on bail for similar previous offences, but in early 1978 they were sent down for terms ranging from eighteen months to two years; and senior CID officers also correlated the resurgence of local street crime during 1980 and 1981 with their resumption of criminal activity after release from imprisonment.

This interpretation could well have implications both for the police attitudes to, and tactics against, crimes of this kind. If, as it suggests, crime levels depend so much upon the activities of so few, this not only makes a mockery of police assumptions that criminality is pervasive amongst black youths, but also casts the gravest doubt on both the point and effectiveness of indiscriminate ('swamp') stop and search police tactics – quite apart, of course, from the ways in which these may generate resentment and impair relationships between police and community.

But the law-enforcement interpretation cannot alone explain the decrease in street crime during 1978 and 1979. Other perspectives crowd in to offer ancillary reasons, notably the 'social prevention' viewpoint which emphasises the value of action to control the number and usage of local squats. In mid-1977, there had been some twenty-six quats on the sub-division, mostly inhabited by 'Dreadlock' groups of West Indian youths who had either rejected, or been rejected by, their families, and whose hand-to-mouth ways of life too often drew them into street robbery and theft, sometimes rationalised as 'survival crime'. In fact, the location of these squats largely coincided with the main areas of street crime – beats 6, 7, 9, and 10 to the south-east of the sub-division – and some squats had clearly become, in effect, bases for offences of this kind, breeding great fear and insecurity amongst the people living round and about them.

To counter this, collaboration developed between police – notably Superintendent Webb – and housing authorities to reduce the number of squats and to regularise conditions of occupancy. Where rent books were issued, occupants were able to claim social security benefits, and this in turn helped to reduce both needs and motives for 'survival crime'. Contact between Superintendent Webb and a local Trust also led to at least one group in a squat being subsidised for 'self-help' activities. Thus in mid-1981 only eleven squats remained on the sub-division, some of them with officially recognised status. Yet although social and crime problems associated with local squats have been effectively reduced over recent years, fresh problems arise as a number of homeless black youths take to a moving pattern of accommodation, temporarily sharing different addresses officially rented by acquaintances. This makes the recovery of stolen property and the arrest of offenders far more difficult for the CID than in the days when they went to certain known squats with some confidence that stolen property and offenders could be found together. Now they spend far more time on following up enquiries that prove fruitless, clear-up rates decline, and their problems are exacerbated as local criminals look further afield, extending their activities beyond Handsworth to out-lying districts of the West Midlands.

And although reduced, problems associated with the squats remain as a sour and common source of local fears and insecurity, the taste of which is given in the comments of a young car patrol constable (15 July 1981):

> 'I went to a burglary this morning down the Lozells Road. An 82-year-old lady had been burgled at 2.30 in the morning, but didn't report it till 8.30 because she doesn't have a phone and was too scared to go out of the house till she thought it was all clear. Two Rastafarian youths had broken in, 14–16 at the very most, and from what they took, it's obvious they're living in squats. They went straight to the pantry and took every item of food she had. About £200 worth, because being an old age pensioner, she doesn't go out much. They would have needed a whole lot of carrier bags to cart it all away. And what got me too was that the neighbours, a young Asian couple, mid-twenties, they knew all about it, they could hear it all going on, and normally they look after this woman, but because they didn't have a phone, they wouldn't go out and report it either. Now this woman, all she had left was 50p in her purse. I would have given her a few quid myself to get food, but we have to report it to the social services. She said "No way do I want the social services, I'm getting my pension tomorrow." But I came back and contacted the social services straight away . . . The thing is, she shouldn't have been put through all that.'

The fact that the resurgence of street crime during 1980 and 1981 has been so very gradual raises added doubts about the law-enforcement interpretation, and gives some weight to 'economic' perspectives, which tend to link that resurgence to

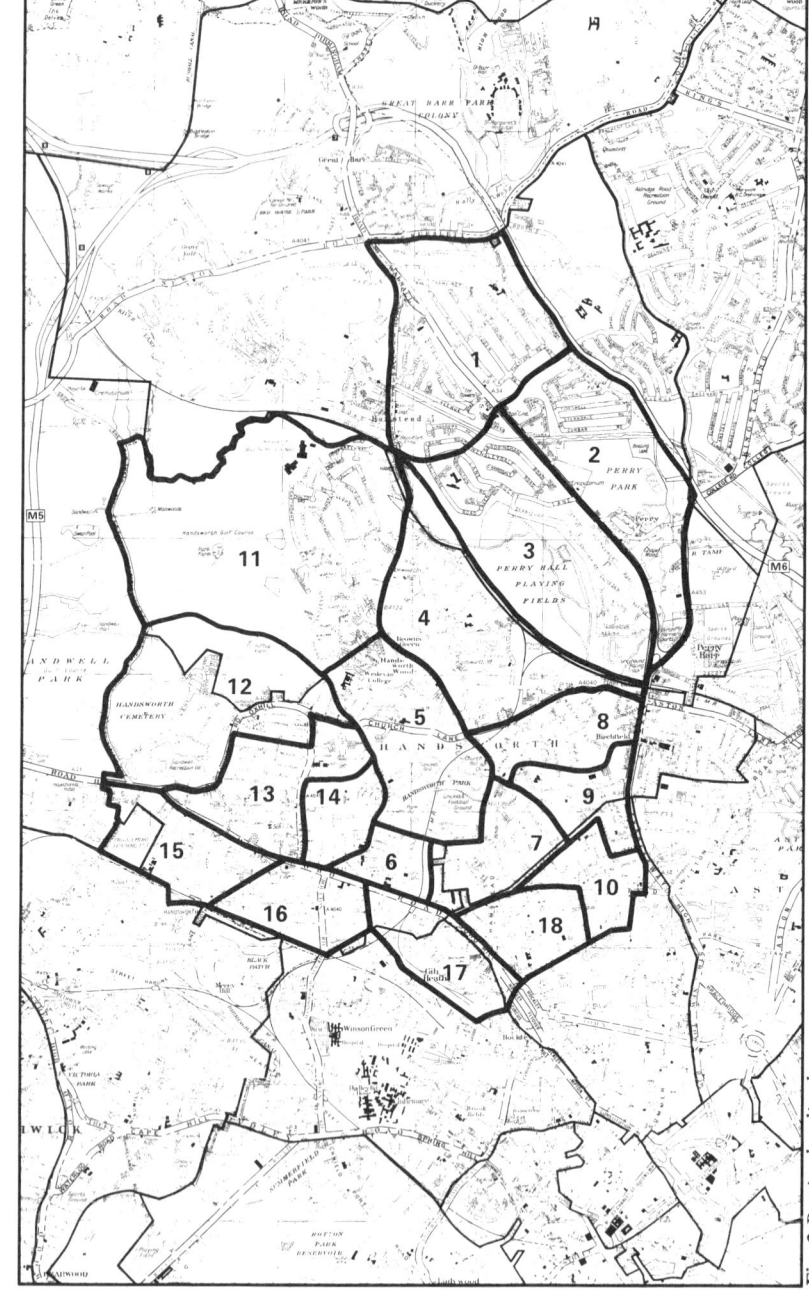

Fig. 3 Revised police beat areas

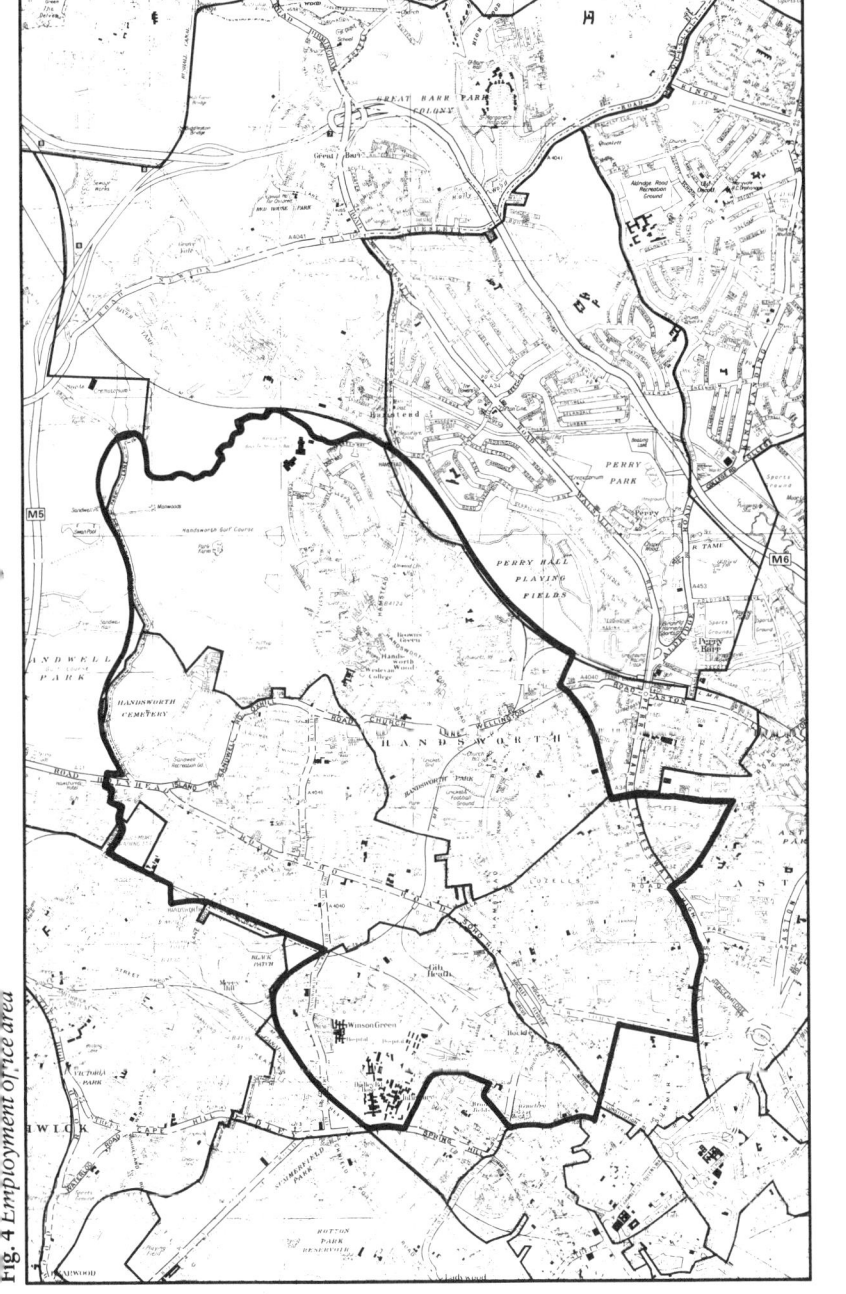

Fig. 4 Employment office area

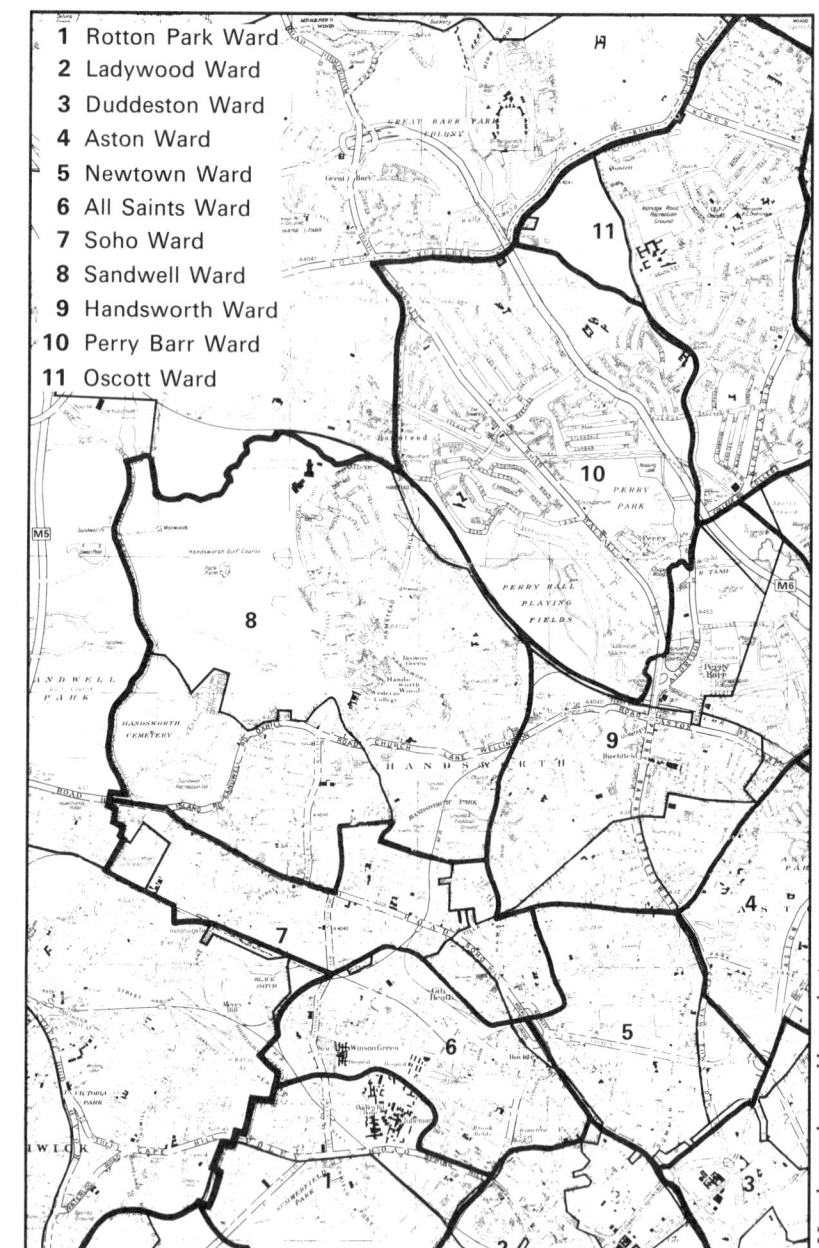

1 Rotton Park Ward
2 Ladywood Ward
3 Duddeston Ward
4 Aston Ward
5 Newtown Ward
6 All Saints Ward
7 Soho Ward
8 Sandwell Ward
9 Handsworth Ward
10 Perry Barr Ward
11 Oscott Ward

Fig. 5 Handsworth ward boundaries

the growing number of local unemployed, particularly young black unemployed, over the same period.

Local vulnerability to unemployment is certainly well attested. In early 1979, for example, a Passenger Transport Executive survey of 1,071 houses in the Handsworth/Lozells area, based on a 20 per cent sample, showed that 60 per cent of the economically active were unskilled manual workers with an unemployment rate of 15.2 per cent, the young and old being most severely affected. In June of the same year, the County Treasurer's Report on Unemployment in the inner areas of the Birmingham Partnership demonstrated both that Handsworth had the highest proportionate concentration of ethnic unemployment in the Birmingham area, and that ethnic unemployment was rising faster than total unemployment in the district.*

Since that time, local unemployment problems have grown radically worse, overall numbers of unemployed people registered at the Handsworth Employment Office during the period under review being as follows:

Date	Under 18			Over 18			Total Unemployed		
	M	F	Total	M	F	Total	M	F	Total
January 1977	182	185	369	3521	1157	4678	3703	1342	5045
July 1977	507	402	909	3428	1176	4604	3935	1578	5513
January 1978	202	177	379	2910	1049	3959	3112	1226	4338
July 1978	396	322	718	2627	1045	3672	3023	1367	4390
January 1979	208	148	356	2699	1105	3804	2907	1253	4160
July 1979	405	335	740	2588	1006	3594	2993	1341	4334
January 1980	235	149	384	2507	1006	3513	2742	1155	3897
July 1980	501	378	879	3419	1405	4824	3920	1783	5703
January 1981	237	168	405	5270	1960	7230	5507	2128	7635
July 1981	438	360	798	6053	2174	8227	6491	2534	9025

---

* NB 'Handsworth' may here be taken to delineate the catchment area of the Handsworth Employment Office, which only approximates to the area of the Handsworth Police sub-division. Both differ considerably from the area of the Handsworth ward. (See maps on pages 70 72 for the relationship between the local police, employment office and ward boundaries.)

Yet in terms of these statistics, at least, links between the numbers of unemployed registered people at the Handsworth Employment Office and the numbers of crimes reported to the Handsworth Police Station over the four years under review are, at best, indirect (see table opposite).

In graphic terms, the relationship between local yearly reported crimes and local recorded unemployment looks like this:

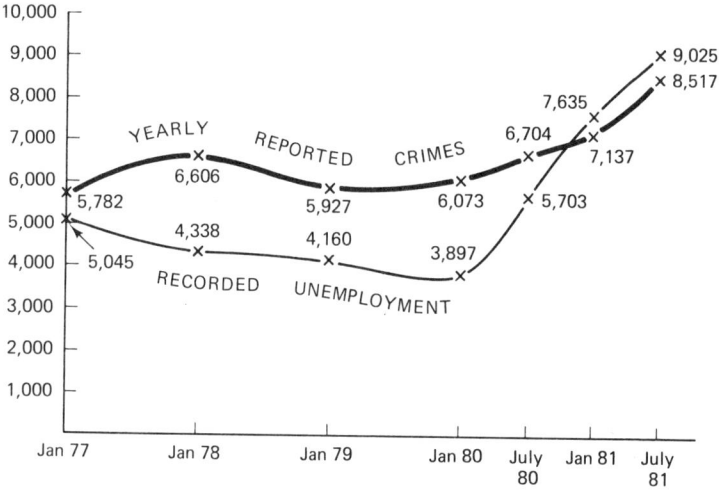

Fig. 6 *Graph comparing yearly reported crime and recorded unemployment statistics*

It would be reasonable to assume that data of this kind, however suspect or 'soft' it might be, could throw light on the effects of unemployment amongst the group most commonly assumed to be at risk – males under 18. Yet the number of under-18 males registered as unemployed at the Handsworth

	Registered Unemployment		Recorded Crime	
	No. of Cases	%	No. of Cases	%
1977	5,045 → 4,338	−14.01%	5,782 → 6,606	+14.25%
1978	4,338 → 4,160	− 4.10%	6,606 → 5,927	−10.28%
1979	4,160 → 3,897	− 6.32%	5,927 → 6,073	+ 2.46%
1980	3,897 → 7,635	+95.92%	6,073 → 7,137	+17.52%
1981*	5,703 → 9,025	+58.25%	6,704 → 8,517	+27.04%

Employment Office *decreased* from 507 in July 1977 to 438 in July 1981 (−13.61 per cent), a period during which reported youth crimes substantially increased.

The official statistics do, however, confirm the unemployment trends among ethnic minorities noted in the 1979 surveys. Comparative analysis of Manpower Services Commission returns of ethnic unemployment in Handsworth for February 1981 reveals a rise of 106 per cent (from 1,811 to 3,732) over the two-year period against a rise of 76 per cent (from 4,338 to 7,635) amongst all unemployed registered there over approximately the same period (January 1979 – January 1981), whilst under-18 ethnic unemployment rose by 101.4 per cent (from 139 to 280) amongst all unemployed under-18s registered there over the corresponding periods.

Of the total ethnic unemployed registered at the Handsworth Office in February 1981, 1,519 (40.1 per cent) were of West Indian origin or descent, 398 of them born in Britain; 1,590 (42.6 per cent) of Indian origin or descent, 101 of them born in Britain; 324 (8.7 per cent) of Pakistani origin or descent, 8 of them born in Britain; 93 (2.5 per cent) of Bangladeshi origin or descent, 6 of them born in Britain; and 97 (2.6 per cent) of East African (mainly Indian) origin or descent, 2 of them born in Britain. Of the registered ethnic unemployed under 18, 153 (81 male, 72 female) – 54.64 per cent – were of West Indian origin or descent, 131 of them born in Britain; and 83 (54 male, 19 female) – 29.64 per cent – of Indian origin or descent, 45 of them born in Britain.

---

* January to July 1981 only.

These statistics, dismaying as they are in themselves, almost certainly underestimate the impact of unemployment on the ethnic minorities of the Handsworth area, and may be notably astray as reflections of local ethnic youth unemployment.

In particular, no one who knows the scale of local West Indian school-leavers during the period under review (averaging about 30 per cent of some 1,400 local school-leavers per year), and who has walked and talked with black youths on local streets and in local houses, is likely to accept the 153 registrations at the Handsworth Employment Office in early 1981 as a wholly reliable indicator of the scale of local West Indian under-18 unemployed, even after taking into account the very high West Indian representation on local Youth Opportunity Programmes (70 per cent – 92 out of 132 placements from the Handsworth Careers Office during 1979 and 1980).[5]

So why don't more register? Discussion on this score with some of the youths, and with other West Indians, suggests that with so few jobs now on offer, their qualifications so limited, and discrimination so marked, many don't think it worthwhile whilst some simply can't be bothered to register at regular times, particularly if they don't have the rented accommodation which could bring them additional social security benefits.* So they make out, as best they can, in one or more of the following ways:

– handouts from friends or from members of communal groups with whom they share resources and/or accommodation;

– handouts from parents, some of whom have put by savings for their children through insurance schemes;

– odd jobs on the informal or 'black' economy, ranging from house painting to childminding;

– private selling of goods they have made or which have come to hand, and of services – parties, sound systems, etc.

– proceeds from petty and other crime.

---

* A number of young people manage to draw social security benefits even though not registered at the Careers Office or Jobcentre.

The consequences are a growing number of young people, often on the move, living semi-dependent hand-to-mouth ways of life in which, as necessity presses, distinctions between legal and illegal become increasingly blurred. Well, you have to survive one way or another, don't you? And look at people like Robin Hood, didn't they do much the same, taking from those who have to feed those who have not? Isn't this understandable, and in an unequal, unjust society, is this really wrong? 'I put it to you: now isn't that right, man?'

In ways such as these, attitudes are justified, values modified, and new norms established – with what implications for society? And this great local energy potential of underemployed young people will be channelled which way?

'Economic' perspectives usually emphasise job creation and provision, particularly for the young, as the essential antidote to crime and disorder; and the problems of young West Indians in Handsworth would certainly be eased if more opportunities for employment were available, or could be created. On the other hand, it would be naive to argue that more jobs must mean less crime and disorder in Handsworth, not least because many young blacks make it plain that whilst they may want work, they are not prepared to swap their present 'survival' ways of life for, say, hard, dirty, regular work in local foundries. So until jobs come along nearer to their own inclinations, closer to their own choosing, significant numbers of them are likely to soldier on much as they do now, living from handout to mouth. Small wonder then, that 'survival' crime ranging from petty theft to street robbery, from shoplifting to burglary, was on the increase in 1981, and is likely to continue so.

Though more Indians than West Indians were locally registered as unemployed in February 1981 – mainly as a result of local foundries cutting staff, closing down, or moving out – the impact of unemployment on the Indian community in Handsworth is far less marked. Discussions with local Indian businessmen suggest that up to a quarter of all Indians in the area are either directly involved in a business or are related to families in business; and that even the unemployed who are not directly supported through family businesses are likely to find a measure of support within their own close family networks.

The perspective of 'culture' is thus of prime relevance in assessing local problems, especially the comparative problems of local Indians and West Indians, groups who ostensibly have much in common both in their motives for coming to settle here and in the circumstances in which they now live.

Most of each group came from disadvantaged lower caste or class backgrounds, possessed very limited education or trade skills, and had very poor prospects in their places of origin – the Jullundur area of the Punjab in the case of most local Indians, and rural areas of Jamaica in the case of most local West Indians. Each group was drawn to Handsworth because it offered jobs – mainly the hard, dirty manual jobs in foundries and other manufacturing industries that the British were no longer willing to do – and accommodation – mainly in the old big Victorian and Edwardian houses which the British were no longer willing or able to keep up as the area slid into social decline, and which were rapidly rented out for multi-occupation by immigrant groups who became, in effect, a new proletariat. (The pattern of immigrant settlement in Handsworth was thus very similar to those in Brixton, London and in Chapeltown, Leeds.) And despite changes of jobs and housing amongst first generation immigrants, the groups continue to inhabit the same local environment – mainly below the line of Church Lane, covering half of beat 5, and beats 6, 7, 8, 9, 10, 13, 14, 15, 16, 17 and 18 (see the map on page 70), and under very similar economic pressures, particularly those of rapidly rising unemployment.

Groups with similar backgrounds of economic and social disadvantage living in similar foreground circumstances of economic and social disadvantage might well be expected to have similar problems of settlement and advancement. Yet the patterns and problems of Indian and West Indian experience in these spheres are, in fact, so disparate as to wreak doubt, if not confusion, in theories of economic determinism. In its economic achievement as in its ability to counter the effects of unemployment, the Indian group advances with far greater cohesion and purpose than the West Indian, despite its additional linguistic disadvantages (Punjabi is still the main family and business language of the Soho Road, and will almost certainly be so for years to come); and this growing disparity of achievement between the two groups also significantly expresses itself in terms of educational attainment and in capability both for care – notably of its youth and elders – and for internal order and discipline. (One-parent families, for example, commonplace amongst West Indians, are still virtually unknown amongst Indians.) Tensions between the groups also grow as the gap in achievement opens up. Amongst young West Indians, in particular, resentment of 'Indians and Indian gold' breeds fast, and may well be an earnest of future conflict.

Disparities of this kind between the two groups living and functioning within the same social/economic context can only finally be explained in terms of difference of culture: 'A man can abandon everything – home, country, land – but he cannot abandon himself, that by which he lives and by virtue of which he is what he is.'[6] And despite a plethora of caste, religious and economic divisions within the Indian community of Handsworth, what marks it off from the West Indian is the essentially *communal* nature of its ways of thought, organisation and action deriving from strong deeply-rooted family and community structures, closely woven patterns of human relationships, and powerful value systems sanctified in tradition.

These are the sources, on the one hand, of the group's economic drive, on another, of its capability for care and order. The longer the group lives here, of course, the more its communal ways of life are challenged, modified and slowly eroded in processes of interaction with the changing culture of British society; and the more it is conditioned by prevailing economic and social circumstances and pressures. Inevitably, therefore, police, social, health, employment and other services – statutory and voluntary – come to deal with growing symptoms of stress within local Indian society, ranging from inter-generation conflicts to marital breakdown, from psychological illness to criminality. Despite these symptoms, however, the nature and quality of its communal culture ensures the Indian community in Handsworth a continuing capability both to advance effectively from its initial status of economic disadvantage, and to care for and order itself in comparatively effective ways.

In some measure, that capability derives from the age old Indian experience of developing strategies of defensive – and largely surface – adjustment to their ruling societies (at first, colonial; more latterly, the host society) in ways which ensure the preservation of their own ways of life and the advancement of their own interests. The traditional success of such strategies makes many older (and wiser?) Indians regret that numbers of their 'emancipated' politicized youth should now sacrifice them for the crude confrontation tactics of white and black political extremists; tactics, they think, which will inevitably create backlash against ethnic minority groups, and thus damage both their settlement and their advancement prospects in British society. Some older heads also hypothesise that the Indian families who show the greatest symptoms of stress and criminality in British society are those either too inflexible to change or too ready to capitulate to it.

Local West Indian capability for care, order and advancement is weaker than that of the Indian precisely because the culture of the group is far less communal in nature as well as less deeply rooted in tradition and less confident of itself. The divisive nature of the 'transplant' plantation societies created in the Caribbean during the seventeenth and eighteenth centuries bred a highly individualised, semi-dependent culture, characterised by loose family structures (slaves being denied access to the marriage ceremony) and weak communal traditions. As these plantation societies declined, so communal structures and traditions began to grow stronger, only to be weakened again amongst those who took the post-war passage to Britain. Here their ways of life have also come under challenge both from the changing ways of British society and from those of their own children, often divided amongst themselves in their search for identity and purpose. In Handsworth, acts of rejection between West Indian parents and their young have become commonplace; and my own experience suggests that they feature heavily in the backgrounds of young West Indian criminal offenders in the area.

All of which also suggests that the perspective of 'culture' is useful not only for defining patterns of settlement and advancement amongst Indian and West Indian groups, and the very distinctive ways in which these are likely to develop[7] – issues which the perspectives of 'class', 'race' and 'colour' tend rather to obscure than to clarify – but also for placing the internal capability for care and order of British communities. Whereas the perspective of 'race' tends to emphasise *distinctions* between British and non-British groups – 'us' and 'them'; or 'black' and 'white' – the perspective of 'culture' enables us to construct a comparative frame of reference within which crucial points of *resemblance* between British and non-British may be more clearly identified. Perhaps the most pertinent for those who work in our institutions of care and order are the resemblances between West Indian and British communities, as our society also loses communal strength in terms of family and community structures, patterns of relationships, attitudes and values.

In brief, 'culture' is here far more relevant than 'race' as a perspective both for assessing current problems and for predicting those to come. Links between youth unemployment and crime rates, for example, will certainly differ considerably between Asian, West Indian and British groups in the area.

In this context, the population shifts that have been taking place in Handsworth during the period under review – of West Indians and whites moving out as new rented accommodation is made available elsewhere, and of Asians moving in – have considerable significance for the directions of local life and the functions of local services.

The 'top end' of the sub-division (above Church Lane) has been least affected by these movements, and remains predominantly white, with bourgeois areas to the west, working class areas to the east, and an increasingly ageing population.

At the 'bottom end' of the sub-division, the southern and western areas, together with the south-eastern area of major housing renewal, have been most affected by processes of 'Asianisation', and these are reflected in registers of live births in the main wards of the sub-division. In 1978, Asian live births represented 65.8 per cent of all live births in the Soho ward, 44.3 per cent in the Handsworth ward and 39.0 per cent in the Sandwell ward. In 1979, the number of Asian live births rose by 11 per cent in the Soho ward, 11 per cent in the Handsworth ward and 19 per cent in the Sandwell ward. This trend continued in 1980, and by now (1981) there are more Asians living on the sub-division than people of any other group.

Local school registers tell a similar tale. For example, whereas in Handsworth Wood Girls (Secondary) School – Church Lane, Beat 5 – West Indian pupils had represented nearly three-quarters of the school population just prior to the period under review, by 1981, 60 per cent of the school population were Asian, and Asian girls made up 80 per cent of 1st form classes.

West Indians remain concentrated to the east of the 'bottom end', predominantly in beats 6, 7, 9, 10, which also continue to be the main areas of street crime (96 cases of street robbery/ theft from the person were reported during 1980 in these four beats – the only beats to average over 20 cases each during the year). And in terms both of overall crime statistics, and of police activity, this south-eastern area of sub-division continues to be the key area of police concern.

In sum, ambiguities crowd in upon almost every perspective on the shifting patterns of the Handsworth scene, now linking, now confounding different angles of vision. Discussion of these perspectives must therefore now be specifically related to analysis of policing policies, and to the ways in which those policies are enacted in practice.

7   *Policing policy*

Policing policy in this complex and changing area during the period under review has reflected the general philosophy of the West Midlands police, and has been strongly stamped by the personality of the sub-divisional commander, Superintendent Webb. In recent years. Sir Philip Knights has put increasing emphasis on the necessity for community-based approaches to policing, and under his leadership, a number of notable initiatives in this sphere have been developed within the force area of the West Midlands police.

The Chief Constable has also emphasised the role of divisional and sub-divisional commanders, in forging links with their own communities. And when Superintendent Webb took over command of the Handsworth sub-division in June 1977, he faced daunting tasks on that score. Street crime, in particular, was breeding fear and insecurity amongst local people. Public order was threatened by demonstrations, confrontations, violence. Police-community relations were marked by tension and distrust. Around these a powerful mythology had been created, on one hand by media portrayals of Handsworth as 'the Angry Suburb', on another by ideological interests which sought to present the area as a model of race/class conflict.

Webb's experience as deputy commander of the sub-division had left him with few illusions about local policing problems:

> 'When I came here as Chief Inspector, the first thing that struck me was the resentment I felt from the residents of Handsworth. You're talking to ordinary people, to shopkeepers, to people out on the street, and you can feel the resentment. You can also see it in the number of complaints against police. You think, "Is it the police who are wrong? Are the police behaving in the ways the people here describe? Or is it the public here who are wrong? There must be something wrong here somewhere."

. . . Then the first months I was here, I was having to go out with the policemen on the streets here to squats to make arrests. We'd be going down there, twenty or thirty policemen to arrest a couple of people in a squat, with half the street out. When a single arrest has to be carried out in a military fashion, there's something wrong somewhere . . .

. . . When you take over as Superintendent, then it's down to you. And when you find yourself confronted with a place where every single problem you could possibly imagine is gathered together in one place, then you have a choice. You can either sit there bemused, and plod along in the old police way, reacting to each thing as it comes along, or you can put your cap on, and think what are the problems here, and how they relate to each other, and how you are going to direct matters to deal with them, and what your overall strategy is going to be . . .

. . . The priority was to get out amongst the people, not just me, but the team of officers working with me, to get out to every single group in Handsworth, in temples, schools, churches., amongst community leaders, teachers, residents' associations, old age pensioners – every single group representing anything in Handsworth. Get out to them. Get feedback of what they think is wrong, and build up a two-way contact with these people so we can do something to put things right . . .

. . . But it's very difficult in a place like this with, say, 250 policemen from all sorts of backgrounds, with all sorts of ideas of their own, doing things in their own way without the slightest conception of how these will affect the overall strategy. And if you go too far one way, you lose your men because they think you are taking a soft option, not understanding what may be the best way to deal with problems. And if you go too far the other way, you lose the community leaders. You're walking a tightrope all the time you're trying to act between your men and the public, trying to balance your strategy . . .

. . . On the one hand, there's the problems with the

police, of encouraging the Inspectors to make their own decisions and to run their own shifts, and to not be dependent. But when something happens, should they ring up the Superintendent and perhaps lose their credibility as supervisors with their men? Or should they go ahead as they think fit and perhaps make a balls-up of the overall strategy? This is always difficult, and what I've tried to do over a period of time is to get them all together, and talk to them as often as I can, about the incidents that have happened, and the ways these could affect what we want to do and what is happening in the community, and about the ways things are going at the moment in relation to what we have got to do in the future, and how best to organise our officers and keep them informed of our strategy . . .

. . . On the other hand, there's the problems of talking to the community, particularly the young West Indians. Whatever you say to them is going back into the community very very quickly, and what you say has got to be genuine and it's got to be credible, because they'll relate it back, and relate it to whatever set of incidents is going on at that moment, or to whatever myths or current stories are floating around – police brutality, harassment, or whatever. If some of the kids say they've been stopped or perhaps mistreated by the police, I never deny this to them. What I do say is: "We are trying to stamp it out. That's the reason for our contact with you. If it happens we want you to believe we'll do something about it." It would be stupid on our part to say it doesn't happen because that's ridiculous and they know it's ridiculous. You'll never get to those people if you behave that way. The only way you can do any good is to admit this does happen sometimes, but that you're trying to do something about it. That's the only way you can do any good, to be honest about it. There's no point in beating about the bush . . .

. . . Some senior officers say it doesn't matter what the public thinks of us. "They get a service from us. They shouldn't be complaining about it. We should be impervious to criticism." That's often been police thinking, and perhaps it's not until we get into critical situations as in Handsworth, that we begin to think more about it. Here we realise that police and community, we've all got to live together, and that if we don't get the mixture right, there's going to be demonstrating, there's going to be knocking on the front door, there's going to be brutality, there's going to be violence, there's going to be a tremendous upset, and there's going to be a lot of outside focus on this place. And I suggest things are moving to that critical level in places other than Handsworth. The warning signs are out . . .*

. . . Some policemen are very short-sighted. The police tasks are very basic tasks: to keep the peace, protect life and property, prevent and detect crime. And you have to do everything you can to achieve these ends, and by bringing about better relationships, improve the possibilities of carrying these tasks. So you can't put barriers on what policemen can do. Let a policeman go to a council meeting, tell them about the needs of local people; to a residents' meeting, explain what we do, tell them the facts of life about their area; to ethnic groups, explain what our policies are, what we're trying to do here, what they can do to help us. And say to them: "We will do what we can. You do what you can. We'll meet again soon and talk over what we've both done in that time." And go on like that, month after month, renewing contact, until people genuinely believe the police are doing something for them . . .

. . . And it's essential for the police commander and his deputy to become involved, not just by sitting in the office and directing things, but to go out personally, to keep personal touch with things. It's good to get a feel of things

---

* David Webb's comments reported here were made well before the 1981 riots.

from other officers because you've to take them along with you, but it's essential you get the feel of things yourself. Some might say that with the other responsibilities of a commander you haven't got time to do it, what with complaints to deal with, paperwork and other things. But people want to see you, to talk to you, and have it from the horse's mouth, what's happening, what you intend to do and so on, to put their minds at rest. And there's no way you can sit back and say, "I'm sorry, I can't go out and get involved in that". You can't afford not to do it. Because you, finally, have to make the decisions . . .

. . . From this police liaison with all these groups, we know what's happening here, what's likely to happen, when and where. We have this two-way contact. So that when something big is going to happen in the area, a march for instance, you've done your homework, you know what the possibilities are, what groups are likely to take part, and you've already got your relationships with those particular groups . . .

. . . One example: in May 1979, the Anti-Nazi League wanted to march against the National Front in West Bromwich. We called all the leaders of the groups together, Asians, West Indians, other agencies and people with a concern for Handsworth, and we had a meeting a week before the march was due to take place. We sat down in a pub and put out pints on the table. They'd seen what happened in Southall, how things had got out of hand with ordinary people becoming involved against the police, and a great deal of bad feeling. And we asked them: do we want that to happen in Handsworth after all the hard work we've been doing and what we've achieved? And there was an immediate response: "No of course we don't. We'd be cutting our own throats." So what are we going to do? We've got very few policemen available to take the march through. There could be a thousand people on the march. What are we going to do?

They said straight away: "We'll come on the march ourselves. We'll be in the front row. We'll keep the march moving. There'll be no disorder. No bricks chucked at anybody. We'll take the march straight through Handsworth and drop out when it gets to West Bromwich." They wanted to show solidarity with the people on the march, but they didn't want to get involved in any disorder. They wanted no part of that . . .

. . . So on the day of the march, we all turned up there. They're all in the front row, or acting as stewards down both sides of the march, all the faces that had been sitting in the pub there. Away we go, and the march goes through Handsworth as sweet as a nut. No problems. Not one arrest. Not one incident of disorder . . .

. . . That's the sort of thing I mean. You build up this relationship through a thousand little incidents during the year, maybe trivial incidents, but through them you create this trust between you, and then when the big one comes, which it probably does two or three times a year, then you handle it . . .

. . . At the same time, you've got to take your men along. It's all right taking the public along, but if you can't take the policemen along, you're wasting your time. I can go to a meeting, for instance, and talk about a project, the way we're operating in Handsworth, the reasons we're doing it, and if my policemen don't go along with that, and resist me, if they go around thumping prisoners, or aggravating people, or walking around surly, or not wanting to take part in the things we're doing on the sub-division, with youth clubs, school projects and so on, then the whole thing will just fall apart. So it's essential to strike this balance between what the public wants and what is good operations in the police sense. It's a very, very hard job.'

In sum, the heart of Webb's approach is that police effectiveness depends primarily on the extent to which police can mobilise community support and active collaboration. Community relations are therefore emphatically *not* a matter to be left to a specialist police department. They are the essence of all police work, the key to operational capability. Issues of 'soft' versus 'hard' policing are thus wholly irrelevant. For Webb, the only valid issue here is that of effective versus ineffective policing. From this perspective, he sees community contact as central both to the work of his officers and to his own community functions.[8]

This community-based approach to policing Handsworth is often viewed more ambiguously by the police than by the community. Two distinct factors come together to divide police on this score. On the one hand, divisions of concepts as to the primary role of the police, and – in particular – about the relationship between responsibilities to enforce the law and responsibilities to keep the peace. On the other hand, divisions of functions between officers serving in different arms of the police service, and the varying pressures to which they are subject in those different functions.

Within the local force, group functions are the main determinants of attitudes to policing, which are also conditioned by the viewpoints of supervisory officers. Since the work of the permanent beat officers centres on community contact, and since their numbers have been reinforced and their role given greater emphasis and backing by the Chief Constable over the last four years, their approach to, and views on, policing are almost wholly community-based.

Amongst the uniformed patrol officers, opinions vary a good deal. Most acknowledge that the trust and confidence generated by community contact have brought them distinct benefits, in particular fewer complaints against them and 'less aggro on the streets, on arrest and back in the station'. Most also recognise the benefits of policing Handsworth with 'tact and discretion; give and take; you soon learn these round here': and this recognition has become more widespread as the numbers of probationary constables decline – from 53 per cent of uniformed constable strength in mid-1977 to 44 per cent in mid-1981 – this decline accelerating in 1980 and 1981 as the West Midlands force recruits up to its manpower establishment.

But uniformed patrol officers also ask themselves: 'In seeking to get the community on our side, are we leaning too far blackwards?' On this question, even small matters can breed great heat, a much quoted bone of contention being the issue of fixed penalty parking tickets on the busy Soho Road.

Many of the offenders are Asian shopkeepers loading and unloading goods at all hours from vans or cars. Most of these shopkeepers are staunch supporters of the police, and have already demonstrated their active co-operation in the mounting of community activities such as the Handsworth Festival, and in the maintenance of public order, e.g. during the Anti-Nazi League March of May 1979. They argue that they would be pleased not to park on the Soho Road as soon as a parking area is created close by. Meanwhile – business is business; and they ask the local police to exercise tolerance and discretion.

For the patrol officers, this illegal parking makes for constant congestion of a main arterial route in and out of Birmingham; and many resent any suggestion that they should neglect what they see as their duty to keep the road clear. This resentment becomes inflamed if Asians invoke the name of 'Mr Webb' in their defence. 'It's then we think: sod Mr Webb. Here's a bloody ticket.' In ways such as these, divisions are compounded within the police organisations as well as between police and community.

Other criticisms of Superintendent Webb are that 'he knows more people on the outside than on the inside', and 'doesn't get amongst the lads enough'. These criticisms are countered by those who work closest to him, particularly the longer serving PCs at Thornhill Road: 'He puts in a lot more time and effort than any other Superintendent I've ever known'; and even more to the point: 'Without Dave Webb, make no mistake, this place would have gone "pop" years ago.'

In terms of local police experience, it is not difficult to understand why some uniformed patrol officers resist or reject Webb's community-based approach to policing. In so many of their contacts with young blacks, they know they will be abused and accused of harassment, racialism, dogged by anti-police mythology, no matter what they do.

'Last week we caught two in a woodshed, 16 and 13. And their sister came, about 18. She caused a lot of trouble, shouting we were going to set them up. Turned out she'd been in for shoplifting three years before. And in the car, you could see, they were very apprehensive. First time arrested. So we tried to explain to them, we don't beat people up. Obviously it has happened occasionally. Now and then, it's going to happen, no one can deny that . . . Well, when we got to the station, they were released. No real evidence against them. But 10 to 1, they'd say they were beaten up, to keep face with their mates. And of course it happens when they're going to cough on their mates. They have to have a reason for that afterwards . . . "I had to split on you. They beat it out of me . . ." ' (M and J, a Mobile Police car team)

Police feelings for victims also has a place here:

'When you see some old lady bleeding in the road, done over by a group of young blacks, you don't have to be racist to want to come down on them. And it's bitter when you nick them on one shift, take them to court the next day, see them bailed, and then arrest some of them again on the next shift for the same kind of offence.'

Feelings of this kind run strongest amongst local CID officers, who see themselves as a clan distinct in function and status within the police tribe, and as the front line in the fight against crime. Their approach to policing is thus almost wholly adversarial in perspective, and it is within their ranks that reservations and criticisms about Webb's approach are strongest.

CID officers mount two main lines of argument. The first asserts that 'the community approach to policing has no practical effects, either in terms of arrest or of information leading to arrests', and that 'the PBOs might as well not exist as far as we are concerned.' The second is more equivocal. It recognises that 'confrontation and conflict have eased over recent years', and reasons that 'since the public are now on our side [issues of

WHY and HOW are quickly sidestepped] it's time to take a tougher line, particularly against the young Rastas'.

CID men also deny suggestions of racism, and many are certainly on friendly personal terms with local West Indians. Their grudge is almost wholly against the Rasta-style youths whom they identify as responsible for most local crimes of violence against people and property, and from whom they themselves constantly endure abuse, obstruction and assault ('My first year here as a detective, I was in hospital seven times'). Often bitterly frustrated in their work (detection rates are 'shamefully low'), CID suggestions for a 'tougher line' include saturation policing tactics, e.g. by the West Midlands Special Patrol Group. This is a course of action that Superintendent Webb has not favoured on the grounds that it is both relatively ineffective – displacing crime rather than clearing it up – and could well have disastrous consequences in terms of police-community relations. Inevitably some CID officers see Webb's point of view as almost akin to betrayal – despite the fact that he has never advocated a 'softly softly' approach to crime detection – and their resentment sometimes spills over into biting personal criticism of their sub-divisional commander.

Local police attitudes to policing are thus plagued by doubt, division and inconsistency, deriving from very different, at times *conflicting*, perspectives on 'policing'. And not least of David Webb's achievements in Handsworth has been his ability to temper extremes, reconcile these different interpretations of 'policing' within a reasonably common frame of reference, and present his policies to the public in the form of a reasonably coherent and acceptable strategy.

8 Police and other statutory services

During the period under review, responsibility for creating links with other statutory services for care and order in Handsworth has lain primarily with the sub-divisional commander, his deputy (Chief Inspector Martin Burton*) and the section of permanent beat officers.

In the months following my 'Shades of Grey' report, several younger experienced officers were added to PBO strength, the beats in the key Lozells area were reshaped to allow an additional (18th) beat area (see the map on page 70) and a supervisory sergeant was appointed to the section. As a result, PBO strength increased from 16 PCs in mid-1977 to 1 sergeant and 20/21 PCs (18 on individual beats and 2 or 3 officers in reserve) from the beginning of 1978. More importantly, from that time onwards, greater emphasis and priority were given to PBO functions, and officers were encouraged to make personal initiatives in every form of contact with local institutional and community groups – in brief, to *make work* rather than to do jobs. The consequences have been major gains in terms both of community and their own perceptions of their worth; and though slighting comments on their functions are still commonplace, notably from CID officers, in general their work has gradually gained recognition and acceptance as professionally relevant within the police tribe.

Most PBOs identify closely with David Webb's approach to policing. 'It was tense until three or four years ago, until Mr Webb came along. His approach has made a vast difference.' Recognising that they themselves have a central place in that

---

* Martin Burton succeeded David Webb as sub-divisional commander at the end of December 1981.

approach clearly gives them fresh confidence in the value of their work. 'Formerly there were a lot of problems, particularly with young West Indians. It seemed very much one side against another, fraught with anger, that sort of thing. Now it has quieted a good deal. Things are easier. I think the work of the PBOs has helped in this.'

Greater purpose and pride of craft thus pervades both their acts and attitudes:

> 'When a PBO is given an area, it's his ambition to see that the area is looked after as well as possible. That means the traditional functions of crime prevention and detection, general enquiry work* and close contact with everyone, everywhere. Anyone can rush round in a uniform, but the real thing is the ability to speak to people at all levels . . . If officers think policing is not about relationships, then they are making a rod for their own backs at a later date.'

The PBO Sergeant appointed in January 1978 was Ted Schuck,† a great smiling, booming barrel of a man; as much at odds with his uniform as in tune with his new role; as much at home in European history as in a Brummie pub; 'a lovely man', many in Handsworth say; and a fine natural teacher.

> 'Mr Webb sent for me, asked if I'd like a job as permanent beat sergeant, then gave me an outline of what he wanted me to do, and what is very unusual, a programme. I found it strange at first. I'd been here since 1965, as patrol sergeant, and then station sergeant. I'd been used to hard policing. Had to rethink my approach.'

Given his nature and his interests, however, Ted Schuck soon realised both the need and the potential for collaboration between police and other professional services, and in particu-

---

* During the period under review, the PBO section carried out an average of 3,500 enquiries per year, 20 per cent of them relating to crime reports.
† Ted Schuck retired in September 1981, having completed thirty years police service, and was awarded the British Empire Medal in the 1982 New Year's Honours List.

lar, the long-term value of closer relationships between local police and local schools.

At the time of his appointment as PBO sergeant, police contacts with local junior schools were reasonably well established and accepted, contacts with local secondary schools far more limited. Emphasis was therefore given to police contact *throughout* school experience, and in his report for the year ending 31 December 1978, Ted Schuck laid down guidelines for this development:

> 'In planning school activities, three important factors must always be considered by the police. Firstly, we are not school teachers. Secondly, whatever degree of activity we are considering in any school, we must have the full support of the headmaster and his staff, and the cardinal rule on this must always be that we go into the school on his invitation. Thirdly, we must also consider that over-activity in any particular school can also do damage to the police image in certain instances.'

That first year, beat officers talked with some 8,000 pupils in local schools, some 11,000 pupils visited Thornhill Road Police Station, discussions on policing themes took place with fifth and sixth form debating societies, and Law and Order weeks were organised in local junior schools. These Law and Order weeks subsequently developed into regular major projects, with programmes of written and art work on policing, reinforced by talks from local beat officers, visits from horse, dog and car patrols and films such as 'Never Go with Strangers', and usually concluding with evening functions at which beat officers meet pupils, teachers and parents. Informal networks of understanding and co-operation have therefore gradually developed, reinforcing the role of PBOs as reference points in their local communities.

Relationships between police and local junior schools were also strengthened by a schools football programme covering the summer holiday period of 1978. Following discussions with Superintendent Webb and Inspector Hawkesford, PCs Shuter, Haste, Bennett and O'Loughlin gained the support of a number of schoolteachers, and involved local junior schools and scout groups in a 'World Cup' knockout competition in Handsworth Park, with trophies presented by football celebrities and senior police officers. This too has developed into a yearly event, attracting an increasing audience of local young people and their parents.

Most beat officers have very close contact with junior schools on their patches.

> 'I go on most of the school outings. Every Wednesday, I take a group swimming, and call in perhaps two or three times a week. Talk to the children. Give them an insight into the police job. Then bring classes round to the station, show them how it works. Let them see the cells.'
>
> 'But is this policing?'
>
> 'It's not policing in the old-fashioned way. But to deal properly with the youth, you have to get to know them, especially with immigrant groups suspicious of police and authority. If you can get on friendly relations with them, you're half-way there. The kids learn to trust you, and often this influences the parents. I know that if I go to any of their houses, I'll get a good reception. If a kid's misbehaving, I can go and see the parents, sort things out before they develop. Usually, they're very helpful and co-operative.'

The speaker here, PC Tony O'Loughlin, much to his surprise, was given a BBC Nationwide Golden Helmet Award in 1980 for his community work, following nomination by the St Mary's Church of England School. 'In all truth, I don't think I'm doing anything more than any other PBO.'

From the beginning of 1979, secondary schools absorbed an increasing amount of PBO time and energy. Voluntary after-school programmes were organised so that pupils could choose the 'Police Service' as an optional subject within the Duke of Edinburgh Award Scheme; and by July 1981, some 600 young people had gained Bronze Awards, and 25 Silver Awards, including this option. Arrangements were also made with the co-ordinators of the Award Scheme so that local groups could use the transport facilities and camp equipment of the Lozells Project to run the 'outward bound' activities of the Scheme.

During the period under review, police contributions to local secondary schools included a wide range of talks and discussions, together with teaching of remedial groups and participation in school camps and other out-of-school activities. The quality of that contact was nowhere better demonstrated than in Handsworth Wood Girls' School.

I first visited the School in 1973, and then occasionally from 1977 onwards. Non-selective in its intake, it has always been a pleasure to go there. A sense of care and order pervades the building, not artificially imposed, but deriving from an ethos commonly accepted and enacted by staff and pupils. The discipline is internal, the atmosphere easy and humane. In the making of this school culture, the primary source has very clearly been the Headmistress, Mrs Clare Hinchliffe,* remarkable in her qualities of compassionate understanding, practical commitment, unillusioned good sense as in her awareness of relationships between school and community. (The School has very strong practical traditions of community involvement.)

'The police are a great help in sorting out the problems. First, with the great throughput of West Indians girls in the mid- and late 1970s, now [1981] with the second wave, the Indians who make up the great majority of pupils – 80 per cent of the lower forms. Apart from their work in the classroom with the girls, there is close liaison with the staff. If a girl gets into trouble, or runs away from home, the police help a great deal. If we have a disco, Sergeant Schuck may be about unseen, in case of trouble. Recently an Asian girl ran away from home, and Ted Schuck was running around the backstreets until the early hours, to all kinds of addresses we thought she might be. He's a very exceptional person, no doubt of that.

* Mrs Clare Hinchliffe MBE, retired in July 1981.

About 1978 we had trouble in class, a kind of restlessness, an anti-spirit, we hadn't had for years. There was trouble from children going to the Summer School and Saturday School for Black Studies. There were some good people involved in these schools but also people who were infecting the youngsters, so that they were anti-parent, anti-police, anti-teacher, anti-school. The feeling was very distinct in the second and third forms, those who hadn't had regular classes with Sergeant Schuck. I pointed out the need for a continuing police involvement. And as a result, from September 1979, Sergeant Schuck has come in on a regular basis, and has contributed to a teaching programme throughout the year. This covers not only matters relating to law and order and problems relating to young people, but also goes back into the history of the migration of peoples. Ted has a marvellous feeling for history, and that's very important to these immigrant children.'

I sat in on several of Ted Schuck's sessions on the criminal justice system, with Form IIIS. Of 32 pupils, 22 were of Indian descent, 8 West Indian, and 2 British. I watched them respond, first to his introductory talk, as entertaining as it was informative, his generalisations always made human, his observations salted by vast personal experience; next, to their own role-playing exercise – a magistrates' court, in which they weighed the issues, made the judgements; finally, to Ted's conclusions, relating the functions of the magistrates' court to those of other courts within the criminal justice system. Alert, bright-eyed, questioning, often bursting with laughter, as wholly engrossed as their two teachers (smiling from ear to ear) sitting in on the session, they ended by demanding a visit to a real magistrates' court. Here learning mingled with pleasure, became a living thing.

'Oh, the course has been very useful, but it's not *just* the classes he teaches, it's that he's always walking up and down stairs, bellowing and laughing. I mean, you can hear his laughter in the next village. And the kids would all be nudging each other, and those who didn't know him by being taught by him, chatted to him in the corridor, or he joined them at a little party or dance, reggae or whatever. So they all knew him by sight, and *certainly* by sound.

I can't exaggerate the importance of this close contact in the formative years. Sergeant Schuck comes regularly every week after school, as well as on Tuesdays and Thursdays, and Miss (WPC) Bamber comes on Tuesday mornings, Friday afternoons and other odd times, and what they do out of school is very important, as it's seen by the girls as an extra, and they lend us equipment we couldn't afford, and go on field courses.

The shame is that we see nothing of all this in the newspapers or on television. The girls were appalled when they saw the television programme on community policing because all the emphasis was on the Rastas. The media only seem interested in conflict. The girls are sick of programmes like this. They say they don't want to show the truth about us. It's always the Rastas. I've told the media about Sergeant Schuck, but they've never used it . . . Of course, you don't get a Schuck every day. It's what he is, what he's learned, his feeling for history . . . When he retires, they should keep him here in Handsworth in an advisory or training role. Because you could send umpteen sergeants into schools, and they couldn't do the job he's done here for so long.'

The most ambitious local police/school initiative has been developed in Holte School as part of the Lozells Project. The programme began in September 1979, and three fourth-year forms were chosen to participate, each for two school periods (one hour) per week throughout the school year. The purpose of the project, as set out by Robert Storr, a Holte School outreach teacher, in his report of January 1980, was 'to improve the relationship between young people and the Police Force', and specifically 'to provide the opportunity for a genuine meeting of the pupils with police officers in circumstances that do not contain the stresses that meeting in other places and other times may have'. Emphasis was put upon the need for close personal contact in small discussion groups, and of the use of outside visits, role-playing exercises and films.

Holte is a mixed, non-selective, senior school of some 1,350 pupils, at the extreme south-east corner of the sub-division – in fact, just over the border between 'C' and 'F' divisional areas of the West Midlands police. A police team of 6 officers – Sergeant Schuck and 5 Constables (3 from the Handsworth Sub-division, 2 from F1 Sub-division) – was allocated by the Chief Constable to co-operate with Robert Storr, in running the programme, under the general guidance of the Head-master, Steve Allatt, and Chief Inspector Burton.

I sat in on several sessions between autumn 1979 and spring 1981: the first, a discussion in small groups on police-community relations. The air was often thick with tension and distrust, particularly around a group of young West Indian girls, 14–15 years olds:

> 'The police tell lies. Like about the police station. They say no one beat anyone up there. But they do.'
> 'Young ones the worst. One call me a black bastard.'
> 'An uncle of mine. They beat him up in the police station. Put a pillow on his head so the mark wouldn't show. Then they flushed his head in the toilet. And charge him with something he didn't do.'
> 'They see a black youth in the street, they stop him. Call him a black bastard. Jump on him. Put him in a meat wagon. For no reason at all. Oh God, oh God, it's true.'
> 'And coppers coming into schools? Is a waste of time.'

Myth or reality, did it matter? The perceptions were there, deeply ingrained, seemingly rooted. Interchanges with the young Brits and Asians was less strained, but it was at best grudging. And when a middle-rank police officer declared that no one was ever beaten up at Thornhill Road Police Station, I saw in all eyes the shutters come down. Blank. End of story. 'The bloody fool,' a PC muttered to his mate; and afterwards, 'there's only one way to deal with these kids. Tell them the truth. Explain how violence sometimes can come about. But tell them too how we try to guard against it.'

Subsequent sessions in 1980 and 1981 – during which the programme was extended to cover six fourth-year forms, each for thirteen week sessions – seemed palpably less tense, though still hard graft, with apathy rather than hostility the main enemy. So given the demands the programme made on police resources, was it really worthwhile? Talking this over with all concerned, my impressions were that the main achievement had been to 'normalise' relationships between police, pupils and teachers to the extent that after two years, police had become an acceptable human presence both in the playground amongst the pupils and in staffrooms amongst the teachers. Given the stresses of the Lozells area, this was a real, if limited, achievement.

But doubts persist on other scores, particularly as to the wisdom of concentrating so much manpower in such a limited way. The pupils in the forms involved in the programme – the least 'academic' of the fourth year – are certainly of key concern both from educational and police points of view. Yet would not understanding be better served by a police presence beginning in, and continuing from, the junior forms, before attitudes harden in myth or experience? The experience of Handsworth Wood Girls' School is only partly relevant here – single sex, half the size of Holte, culturally more of a piece, in a less tense environment – yet the objectives of the two pro-grammes are essentially the same: to make long-term invest-ments of manpower directed towards the sovereign police purpose – to keep the peace. And viewed in that context, the case for creating a *continuous and sustained* police presence in key senior schools becomes ever more convincing.

Closer relationships with local schools have led to closer collaboration with the Educational Welfare Service. In November 1979, that Service opened new offices in the Soho Road, regular consultation with the police quickly developed, and thereafter the joint scheme known as 'Citizen 80'. Groups of youngsters aged between 11 and 14 with problems such as high truancy rates, anti-social behaviour and involvement in petty crime, some of them officially cautioned by police, are taken into this scheme on the recommendations of their schools and the Educational Welfare Service. The Scheme has two parts, both taking place in the school holidays: the first, a week's course at Holte School on the roles of various services in society; the second, a five-day camp in the countryside, with activities to encourage group responsibility. Police officers, cadets, education welfare officers and suitable volunteers attend these camps. Twenty-five youngsters took part in the first year, and seventy-five in 1981.

Perhaps the most surprising – and therefore heartening – facet of inter-agency collaboration in Handsworth has been the measure of accord, interchange and co-operation developed between local police and social services, professions often notably at odds with each other in ethos, perceptions of their roles, and not least in tribal loyalties.

> 'Back in 1978, all the services tended to typecast each other. Unless you actually knew whoever it was at the other end of the 'phone on a personal basis, you immediately typecast him or her. The social services had the police down as brutish, reactionary hefties, and the police had the social services down as tinkering, intellectual lefties . . . So when contact was established, we realised how much we had in common as people and in the work problems facing us here. After all, three-quarters of our work as police is concerned with social rather than crime problems.' (Ted Schuck)

As always, interchange developed on the initiative of a few key people on both sides. In the sphere of cautioning policy and practice, for instance, Derek Leigh, a senior social worker responsible for court liaison, made contact with Detective Inspector Vic Green. At first, they discussed cases by telephone, later (1978) at weekly meetings in Thornhill Road Police Station. Information was freely exchanged on both sides as mutual trust grew, case reviews were made more sensitive and more thorough, quarterly forums were arranged at which police, senior social workers and probation officers could discuss general issues about the cautioning of juveniles, and police cautioning policy became far more flexible.

In mid-1979, Derek Leigh commented to me that

'the only children they [the police] don't refer to me now are children they would oppose bail for. The rest, I get full details of the offences well in advance of court appearances. Social workers can thus be informed very much earlier. It's a very big step forward.

This has followed a long period of co-operation with DI Green, and I think he's been interested, and at times surprised, by what we've been able to tell him about the backgrounds of some of the children appearing before the court. I'm sure he's very much more aware now both about their backgrounds and their problems. And I do think that at Thornhill Road as a whole we have a remarkably enlightened body of men, and I've no doubt that Dave Webb is responsible for much of that by passing down his feelings to the officers as a whole. When I've occasionally given talks at Tally Ho (the West Midlands Police Training School) about the role of the social services, I've been surprised by their very hard-line attitudes in contrast to those of policemen at Thornhill Road. We have a different quality of relationships with them there, even though we've had our disagreements, in particular with some of the detectives who tend to be more hard-line than any of the others.

On the matter of police training, there have been small but significant improvements in that all probationary constables from Thornhill Road spend a week at the Community Liaison Office on Hollyhead Road, and for one day of the week they come here, and we show them the things we do, and the sort of people who come here asking for help. That day, for most of them, is quite an eye-opener. We've had about thirteen of them over the last twelve months and only two were not favourably disposed towards us when they left – or at least, that's the impression they gave . . . Longer attachments, of course, would be a great advantage. I think all policemen would benefit from spending three weeks in the local social services office, as policewomen used to do when they were a separate body, if possible in the local office with whom they'll have to work, so that they can build up links and put faces to names.

On the issue of social work attachments with police, well, my own background gave no indication I'd get on with policemen. I was a revolting student like the rest. Hit over the head by policemen on horses in Grosvenor Square. Searched for drugs at parties when I was at college. But I've been really impressed by the openness of the police at Thornhill Road, and it's been through contact with them that I've changed my approach to them, and have arranged for other social workers to have the benefits of meeting policemen. So we've arranged day attachments for them at Thornhill Road, and so far about twenty social workers from this office have shared the experience of policemen there. Now we've a standing invitation to go back, and to go out on the unit cars at night. And all of us who have gone through the experience enjoyed and benefited from it.'

Relationships between police and the local social services department (Centre 3) continued to grow both more cordial and more effective. Terry Jinks and Detective Chief Inspector Harry Udall took over and further developed the collaborative work on young offenders begun by Derek Leigh and Vic Green. From this involvement each gained not only greater mutual respect and understanding of each other's roles, but also greater commitment to the principles of inter-agency collaboration.

In the autumn of 1980 discussions led to group work for young people who had been formally cautioned at Thornhill Road. The leader, Rodney Reed, the Centre 3 intermediate treatment officer, subsequently reported (on 15 July 1981) that 'the excellent working relationship that existed between Centre 3 and the police at Thornhill Road facilitated the organisation of the group'. The scheme was thus quickly put into practice, and activities for a racially mixed group of some ten to a dozen 13–15 year olds, meeting two hours per week, have included community work; training in social skills; literacy work; films, youth club activities; and sporting outings. A residential week-end camp has also been organised.

In addition to Rodney Reed, the project has been staffed by a social worker, a probation officer, a volunteer group worker and a PBO. The latter (PC Tony O'Loughlin), though at times bemused by aspects of the social skills training and by the jargon of staff discussions, has taken on this new role with his customary willingness and good humour: 'Not least of all, for the ways in which it links with the Lozells Project, and it brings police and social workers together as never before. Imagine, three or four years back, us talking, even recognizing each other, let alone working and going out drinking together.'

The relationships are not always so rosy, of course. Tribal insularities persist, on both sides, some grounded in professional ideology, some simply deriving from fears of being *seen* to be closely identified – what would the clients think? But practitioners on both sides are at one in thinking that resistance to collaboration with police is a good deal stronger amongst local probation officers than amongst social workers.

This is quite contrary to most police expectations, which were mainly based on assumptions about the relationship of the two services within the criminal justice system. Yet it is precisely this factor which often seems to impel probation officers consciously to distance themselves from police, and to insist on the essential *independence* of their functions. In contrast to social work functions, which extend across the whole gamut of social needs, probation work functions are largely offender-centred. Probation officers therefore very naturally seek to identify with the needs of their clients as fully as possible. Since hostility to, and resentment of, police burns strongly in many of those clients, particularly young West Indians, it is understandable that some probation officers come to fear that contact or communication with police might serve to compromise the relationships they seek to develop with their clients, and thus compromise their professional role.

In discussions with a small group of local probation officers, at least one made it clear that he eschewed any form of interchange with police. But would it not help him to have information from the police about the *quality* of particular offences? 'Possibly it would. But to lift the phone, to talk personally with police, in doing that, I'd feel I'd betrayed my client, betrayed the trust between us.' But supposing that information could be supplied to him, say through someone with an official liaison function? A long pause. 'Well, perhaps yes . . . that might be acceptable.' There was clearly no point in going further. All before us lay the quicksands of professionalism.

In ways such as these, doubts and uncertainties crowd in on issues relating to interchange with police, human sympathies often at war with objective analysis, some probation officers divided by professional, some by political, ideologies. Yet there is a reverse to this coin – an effective local Victim Support Scheme which has grown out of very sympathetic collaboration between the probation service and the police, the key figures here being Wendy Dale (probation) and Martin Burton (police), the latter acting as temporary chairman until the scheme got under way.

> 'It's essentially a probation service function, but a function that cannot succeed without the support of the police. Every day our collator sifts the information at his disposal, and refers to the probation offices those cases he thinks are suitable for members of the Victim Support Scheme to visit. The types of crime we deal with are not those for which an agency already exists, such as rape or wife-battering. And because of their very nature, sexual crimes are out. But victims of other crimes, robberies, thefts, housebreakings and so on, especially the elderly, receive visits from our helpers.
>
> The Scheme started on 1 May 1979, mainly financed by the Cadbury Trust. And we now [July 1979] have about thirty trained helpers. They go through a course of instruction organised by the probation departments. The

sort of help they give is mainly by way of advice, comfort and support. Not only to help people cope with the effects of their experience, but also, for instance, to assist them in making a claim to the Criminal Compensation Board, or when they have to go to an identity parade, or to appear in court . . . And this is not only useful in itself, it has also had the effect of improving relationships between the probation service and the police.'

Wendy Dale saw the scheme in a similar light.

'As we began to work together, we decided to go out for a day with the police, and they would spend a day with us. I was the first to go out with a beat officer for the day. It went very well. I began to see a different side of police work. And now we're making sure our students go and see the police . . . We mix a lot more now, although I think the probation office worries more about the confidentiality involved in having police officers with us, than the police worry about us coming with them . . .

There's got to be a build-up of trust between us. We haven't had much luck with the CID yet. And certainly our clients complain most about them. When I first started here [1977], most complaints were about the uniform branch – about young people challenged on the street, threatened or beaten up, or parents being kept from seeing their children, things of that kind. But with the uniform branch, things have really improved now. And the Victim Support Scheme has helped things a lot.'

Ambiguities of professional attitudes also surround the Lozells Project, the major inter-agency initiative deriving from planning meetings in December 1978 and April 1979 between the Chief Constable, the chief officers of the West Midlands Education, Probation and Social Services, and representatives of the Birmingham Inner City Partnership. These meetings defined both the location and the aims of the project – to reduce crime and vandalism; to develop closer links with the local community; and to encourage people living in the area to participate with local agencies in the solving of community problems. A grant to the project of £50,000 a year was agreed, costs to be shared by the Birmingham Inner City Partnership and the West Midlands police in the ratio 3:1.

Suitable premises were sought for a centre in which officers from the police and other statutory agencies could work with other volunteers to develop a programme of community activities, in particular for young people in the Lozells area; and funds were meanwhile made available for associated community activities and to purchase suitable transport (mini-vans) for visits and outside sporting and camping activities. A local Steering Committee was set up under police chairmanship, including representatives from statutory and voluntary services, and several funded projects began in September 1979, including a social services play scheme, a probation service community workshop, and an education service school toybank, as well as the Holte School project quoted above. The Warden of the Centre (Mike Dobson, an ex-teacher) was also appointed, though the opening of the Centre itself (the Wallace Lawler Centre, close to Holte School) was delayed until September 1980. The timetable of centre-based activities in the first period of full operation (autumn 1980 to spring 1981) is given in Appendix A.

Youth club activities have a central place in the programme, the Junior Youth Club (8–12 year olds) meeting between 4 and 7 p.m. each Monday and Thursday, and the Senior Youth Club (13–17 year olds) between 7 and 10 p.m. on the same days. By spring 1981, the average attendance was about 50 in the Junior Club, and about 80 in the Senior Club, rather more than half of them of West Indian descent (Asians were predictably few), and some 40 per cent of them girls. Activities included table tennis, pool, darts, small games, table football and snooker, a football team was in process of formation, and other outside activities were being planned. Whenever I visited the Club, the atmosphere was busy and pleasing, free and easy yet well-ordered.

The development of youth club activities in this first phase of operation has depended mainly on the work of the Warden and a regular team of PBOs. They have been assisted by volunteers from youth and social services, and Superintendent Webb has also required Unit police officers to attend sessions on a rota basis, to share the experience of local youth in non-conflict circumstances. Police involvement has thus been dominant, and though extremely useful, this has at times proved a source of tension in relationships with the Warden, with other local youth organisations, and with volunteers from other services.

By early summer 1981, however, relations between the Warden, the PBO team and the youngsters in the Club were clearly far more harmonious and more effective. PBO officers such as PCs Lay and Gerrett, and WPC Bamber, were working regularly in the club with considerable sensitivity, commitment and initiative. Most of the youngsters seemed happy and enthusiastic. Activities were beginning to flourish. Many parents in the area were expressing approval.

Yet criticisms persisted, questions multiplied, on several scores. Was it right or appropriate to use untrained policemen in 'professional' youth club work? Were resources being given to the Wallace Lawler Centre at the expense of other local youth activities? Was the Lozells area being favoured at the expense of other equally needy areas of Handsworth? To what extent was the Lozells Project serving those most at risk in the area? And to what extent was this a genuine multi-disciplinary initiative, to what extent simply a police project?

In answer to this questioning and criticism, Superintendent Webb and others on the steering committee have sought to integrate Wallace Lawler Youth Club work more fully into the pattern of local youth organisation activities; to ensure that Lozells Project funding is extended to a wide range of local group functions, both statutory and voluntary (including the purchase of office equipment for a Rastafarian self-help group); and to extend the Lozells Project activities into other areas of Handsworth, notably through the formation (autumn 1981) of another youth club at Westminster Road School, nearer the centre of the sub-divisional area. In ways such as these, despite the ambiguities of professional and community attitudes, the Project has been increasingly shaped to local needs.

At the end of the period under review, I talked over local policing developments with two senior members of staff of Centre 3 Social Services, both of whom had been in constant contact with police throughout the period, and were closely involved in collaborative projects:

> 'Before David Webb took over, the police were losing the support of a large number of the adult community, a very serious situation for them. Without that support, the police can't do their job. In any incident at that time in which police were involved, there was always the potential for explosion.'

Both quoted characteristic examples:

> A young constable dealing with a Rastafarian youth on the streets, asserting his authority, the young West Indian becoming excited and emotional.
> 'Don't tell me what to do. I can stand here if I want to.'
> 'Come on laddie. Get a move on.'
> 'Man, get your hands off me.'
> The young policeman feeling his authority threatened in front of the public, feeling he must be seen to be obeyed. The young West Indian burning with resentment with what he sees as injustice. The whole thing escalating out of all proportion . . . From incidents like this can come violence, charges of assault on police, sometimes with tragic consequences for the youth involved. And as the stories went round, often exaggerated in the telling, the parents came less and less to believe in the police.
> Things are now much better. They have improved quite substantially as a result of David Webb's involvement.

Both also quoted examples of that involvement: the Superintendent contacting the social security office to ensure that a West Indian youth could draw benefits; liaising with the

Housing Department to get squats regularised; negotiating with Trusts to get grants for Rastafarian groups:

> 'But he has a problem now. How does he keep up the momentum of his changes? How does he carry his own officers with him? How does he maintain the balance between enforcing the law and keeping the peace? After the Brixton riots [April 1981] police throughout the country have to find this out.
>
> In Handsworth, David Webb has done a tremendous job in helping to move things towards consensus rather than conflict. It's significant that the political extremists there have made no ground at all in recent times. All credit to the police that they have been able to defuse sources of conflict before they could turn nasty.
>
> At the same time, we have been concerned at some aspects of the Lozells Project. Though we fully support the project, it would certainly have got off to a better start if there had been greater consultation between police, other agencies and community groups at grass-root level during the formative stages of the project, so that it could have grown out of local needs rather than appearing to have been imposed from above. And then it would also have been seen as a truly collaborative venture rather than the police in the forefront.
>
> But in all fairness to the police, they've shown themselves more and more willing to accommodate the views and advice of other agencies and community groups as the project has developed. They've come to learn what we've all had to learn in Handsworth: to work co-operatively. To recognise that the best strategy to tackle local problems is by joint decision-making, with inputs from as many local groups as possible. And this also represents the best use of manpower resources.'

To achieve collaboration of this kind, they recognised, was no easy task. Common problems and priorities for action had to be clearly identified, and the respective roles of the various agencies clearly defined:

'And in order for there to be closer relationships and better co-operation, differences will have to come out . . . At the moment, there are some exchanges between us and the police at Thornhill Road. New policemen come here for a day. New social workers go there for a day. These are valuable, but they're not enough to ensure mutual understanding. We're still too isolated from each other. Attachments for a week rather than for a day would have far greater effect.'

Summing up, what then was needed to ensure more effective collaboration between police and other agencies? At a general level, they suggested, was a prime need for changes of attitude to collaboration within the police service with a more positive lead from senior officers.

Opportunities for sharing the experience of other agencies and local communities, particularly during training, should also be radically extended, so that police horizons could be stretched beyond the insularities of their own institutions, and officers could come to understand how their functions should and could connect with those of other organisations.

At local level, resources should be sought for genuine inter-agency projects, involving both statutory agencies and community groups, with no one interest dominant. This would allow more credible, flexible and experimental approaches to local problems, ensure better co-operation between groups, and provide more effective services.

In ways such as these, they thought, police would come to a fuller understanding both of the need to work with and through communities and of the ways to do so: 'After the Brixton riots, the police have to rethink on these lines. There is really no other practical way.'

9 *Police and community*

Closer relationships with other agencies serve to extend relationships within the local community. The process is two-way. Growing contact with teachers, youth, probation and social workers, housing and employment officers, leads on to growing contact both with those they serve – victims of crime, children and parents, young offenders and others at risk, disadvantaged groups and so on – and with those at places which they frequent or where they meet and congregate – shops, pubs, clubs, temples, churches, community organisations of all kinds. And growing contact of this kind, in turn, strengthens and renews contact with local public services. In ways such as these, formal and informal networks of care and order are created and reinforced. In consequence, the police (primarily the PBOs), whose functions draw them into this web of relationships, come increasingly both to conceive and to enact 'policing' as something you do *with* others rather than *to* others, as a process of *long-term interaction* rather than as a series of short-term actions.

For this perspective on 'policing', some younger PBOs judge much of their training school experience to be, at best, irrelevant:

> 'At training school, we were mainly taught about our powers under the law, and how best to handle certain situations – for example, how to get somebody into custody who doesn't want to go there. It didn't prepare us at all for policing a multi-racial area like this. We've had to learn that here, from our own experiences on the job.'

This viewpoint is often reinforced by more experienced officers:

> 'Training is all too much about powers, what you can and can't do, how to feel collars. So when the young coppers come here, they think that's what policing is all about.

> They haven't been taught how to use their eighteen pence-worth of common sense, how to approach people, how to talk to them. And to cover up their lack of confidence and knowledge, they tend to go at it like a bull at a gate.'

Even with appropriate training and experience, the central police task of keeping the peace in Handsworth is formidable. Threats to the public tranquillity come from so many sources – criminal, political, commercial, professional, racial, cultural, religious, caste, family and personal amongst others – and since violence is just as likely to erupt *within* as between groups, whether white youth cults, Asian families or Rasta sound systems, local patterns of division and conflict are infinitely more complex than the simplistic class/race conflict models of political and sociological theory.

In coping with this task through their day-to-day dealings with individuals and groups, organisations and businesses, on their beats, PBOs show the same kind of skill and commitment as in their dealings with other statutory services:

> 'It's no good just having a policeman out on the streets. It's got to be an experienced policeman who understands the attitudes and problems of the people on his patch, and who's in constant contact with them.' (Ted Schuck)

In busy commercial areas like the Soho Road, constant contact with local businesses – shopkeepers, publicans, market traders – is seen as a necessity on both sides:

> 'Most shopkeepers will tell you, the best insurance a shopkeeper can have is a policeman going into his shop on a regular basis. Because the public get to know. To my mind it's essential that shopkeepers are looked after. Now take that shop we've just been in – the shoe shop – the manager there doesn't believe in relief managers so when he goes on holiday, one of the girls is left in charge. They're a bit concerned about taking the cash to the bank in the evenings, so we go along, and if they are worried, we help them along to the bank.'

Shopkeepers respond warmly to this preventive and deterrent presence, now more regular and therefore more effective than before:

> 'The police are very good, always in and out, asking "Everything alright. Any problems?" I say, would you like a coffee, and sometimes it's yes, sometimes no . . . At times in the past, I used to dread coming through the door, especially Saturdays. We'd get groups of youths in here, it wasn't just their attitude, but they'd come in half a dozen at a time, then all of a sudden you'd see only four, and two would be round the back, or upstairs. Know what I mean? . . . The police have done a fantastic job in quieting things of that kind down. Charlie [PC Charlie O'Donnell] for instance, he's helped a lot, and he gets on great with everyone round here . . . Even walking the streets at night, that's easier now. A few years back, I wouldn't have walked round here at night. I wouldn't. But the last two Tuesdays, for instance, I've had a night out here with some of the West Indian chaps that come in the shop.'

PBO contact has also been strengthened with the ten to twelve residents' associations active in the area during the period under review. Between the beginning of 1978 and the end of 1980, PBOs attended 209 of these meetings, the numbers of people present at each varying between 10 and 300. This has enabled police to stay closely in touch with grassroots circumstances and needs, to deal quickly with complaints, and to help tackle or defuse street-level problems. It has also furnished opportunities for consultation with local planning and environmental health officers, local councillors, and others attending such meetings – occasionally local MPs.

In several areas, these forms of community contact have been supplemented by mobile police offices set up and manned by beat officers; and they are also reinforced by regular visits to the local British and West Indian churches, local Sikh, Hindu and Ravidass temples, and local West Indian, British and Indian social and community organisations. As a result, interchange and interaction between police and community has developed to such a point that, in Ted Schuck's words, 'it is very rare that any meeting of significance takes place without the sub-division being notified'.

In brief, the PBO section has done much to give flesh and blood to concepts of a community-based policing strategy, and to extend and develop the local network of sustained personal contact which alone generates effective interaction between police and community. In so doing, the PBO section has done much to reinforce the network of contact created by the sub-divisional commander and his deputy.

The extent to which David Webb has practised what he preaches during the period under review is certainly reflected in the exceptional range and depth of that community contact, the base for a growing pattern of police-community interaction remarkable in a multi-racial urban area of this kind. To create this, Webb has made himself available to the people of the area at virtually any time and place – in meeting halls, offices, front parlours, temples, churches, shops, cafes, pubs, clubs, squats and cellars, as well as in the police station, on the streets, and often in his own home – in brief, whenever and wherever local people gather for whatever purposes.

To walk the streets and frequent the meeting places of Handsworth with Webb, as I have done continually over recent years, is to be constantly waylaid – often every few yards – by individuals and groups seeking contact, consultation, advice on a host of matters, personal and collective, ranging far beyond the call of police duties. Almost wholly unrecorded, and therefore rarely acknowledged within the service, these contacts, in fact, constitute the cornerstone of Webb's effectiveness as a police commander. From them derive the trust, confidence, and co-operation which enable him to enact his many influential roles in Handsworth. Now as adviser on community policies. Now as moderator in community dialogue. Now as catalyst for community actions. Now as mobiliser of community resources for care and order. Now as mediator in community conflict, both between and within groups. Almost, at times, as local ombudsman.

His community involvement thus extends into areas which many policemen would simply dismiss as 'not police business' – e.g. resolving conflicts of interest between rival groups of Asian shopkeepers at odds over wholesale/retail practices; advising Rastafarian groups on self-help developments; acting as 'honest broker' in Asian family disputes when marriage arrangements break down; aiding the development of local job creation and leisure facilities. Yet it is precisely this measure of involvement, or more properly, this total 'immersion' in the community, which gives him the capability not only to anticipate, prevent or defuse potential threats to the peace of an area in which political/social militancy is ever active, but also to respond appropriately and with confidence to incidents which do arise, thereby avoiding the pitfalls of 'overpolicing' tactics. In brief, Webb's effectiveness as a police leader is rooted in his achievement of having made himself a central reference point for community thinking and action.

Blacks, whites and browns – rather more than blues – attest the value of this work from many angles of vision. Assessments by local social, religious, business and community groups are, in general, wholly supportive of Webb's approach, echoing the comments of Tulsi Thukral, a Vice-Chairman of the Birmingham Community Relations Council, with substantial trading interests in Handsworth:

> 'We have now a good relationship with the police. They are helpful to us, and we are helpful to them. There are difficulties from extremists who have come and started offices here. They want to create something for themselves. But we, we wish to maintain peace, and law and order . . . I think of some years ago, when David Webb first came, he started to understand the problems here. He listened, even to the ordinary people who had difficulties. And now, along with his deputy, he is doing a marvellous job . . . They have put extra men on the beat, and this has helped a lot. Previously, some youths used to follow shoppers all the time, to snatch purses and bags and run away. But now it is not happening so much like that . . .

But not all his junior staff have this understanding yet. I hope that gradually by mixing with others, and through the persuasion of the senior officers, they too will come to understand, and to do a good job.'

Any reservations that local 'establishment' figures have about Webb's strategy seem mainly centred on their wishes for harsher, more repressive, policies and practice against the Rasta-style youth whom they identify with the worst of local crime. This is a viewpoint most strongly expressed by older West Indians, who feel that such youths sully and betray the community reputation of their countrymen by both their criminal activity and their seemingly work-shy attitudes to life.

Indian community leaders are predictably most wholehearted in their approval of Webb's policies. Those with commercial interests, of course, have a major vested interest in keeping the peace, but can also speak with conscious pride in what has been created between police and community in Handsworth :

'When you go outside Handsworth, and ask any police officers, "Let us talk this matter. Let us get together both parties," he will say "That is not your job. That is *my* job. If somebody bent, I put them in Court. Why should I waste my time, talk to this party, talk to that party. Cause myself botheration?" But here, if something come up, we have the courage to talk to each other. If we think something going to develop, we try to find out root cause. And then we try to see if there is possibility to tackle this problem together. Here we use the police as peacemakers, not as trouble-makers. And that is only due to Mr Webb's efforts . . . Community can only have trust in police if police are listening to their problems and giving them good advice to solve them. This type of relationship we already have in Handsworth. And sooner or later we must have it in other areas. God knows how long it will take.'

A significant consequence of the trust generated by sustained personal contact between police and community is that towards the end of the period under review several local Indian leaders expressed a clear preference for *informal* rather than formal methods of making complaints against police:

> 'When we have complaint against police, we like best to go there to police station, talk it over. If we make official complaint, then that complaint, it is dealt with by police authority. That is not the way out. Automatically they will support own people. No, to make complaint in writing is not sensible way. Sensible way, that is just to pass on information to superiors, leave them to talk to their officers.'

But it is amongst West Indian community leaders that attitude changes towards local police have been most clearly apparent during the period under review. In the 1970s, few were more consistently or militantly critical of police performance than James Hunte, now a Labour councillor, and a member of the West Midlands Police Authority. As one whose community work keeps him in constant contact with local police, he knows well what has come to pass on the sub-division:

> 'Webb has done more than anyone deserves to ask of him. He's worked hard. He knows the area. He knows its various problems. But how much further can he go without greater recognition or support from the police? If I were him, I would have resigned long ago . . . But who can follow him? The problem that really concerns me is that of continuity.'*

Hunte's reservations about Webb's achievement differ considerably from those of most other local leaders, but offer a valid critical perspective. They centre on the fact that under Webb's leadership, police-community tensions and conflicts

---

* James Hunte's comments quoted here were made in May 1981, nearly six months before Superintendent Webb's retirement from the police service.

have been reduced to such an extent as to mask the innate social/economic/racial tensions of the area, and the conditions of radical disadvantage which give rise to them. In his eyes, this may have served to hold back investment and development in the area. He therefore stresses the need for 'real social policy in the area, not just police provision. We have to relate police policy to social and economic policy.'

Officials of the West Indian Federation Association commented (May 1981) on similar lines, 'There's some justification for young people being anti-police because of experience in the past that they or their friends might have had of police brutality. But now the police are taking a much more positive approach.' In consequence, interchange and collaboration with the police have swiftly developed, with joint discussions on local needs and projects, and meetings to create dialogue between young West Indians and local police officers: 'When you get to know policemen personally, it plays a big part in creating trust and confidence.' The General Secretary of the Association, Lloyd Blake, made it plain that

> 'Superintendent Webb has my full backing for what he's doing. He's created understanding. He's helped develop useful, practical projects and so on . . . But there's still a lot that local and central government must do to improve the lot of West Indian youths. We don't want violence here like that in Bristol or Brixton. What we want here is political action to alleviate the problems of our young people, in particular the young Rastafarians.'

He recognised certain central difficulties: on one hand, the piecemeal nature and purpose of services, statutory and voluntary, currently responding to the needs of young blacks; on the other, the lack of coherent purposes and organisation amongst Rastafarian groups, often at odds with each other, not least on issues as to whether, or to what extent, they should opt in or out of society. Yet some of these groups had already given evidence of considerable creative skills, especially in terms of the arts and crafts; and he saw urgent need for policies to provide them with the springboard facilities and resources which would enable them to set up their own self-help economic ventures in which they could mobilise and develop these creative skills and market the products of them.

One Rastafarian group with whom I talked was already making plans on these lines, and was seeking premises for a workshop where arts and crafts skills could be taught and put to practical effect ('We have the people to teach woodwork, drawing, all sorts of skills: qualified people who can't get jobs'); where a counselling service could be established; and where social and cultural activities could take place. Their project had drawn them into contact with Superintendent Webb; and he had talked matters over with them – much as he had been doing since mid-1979 with other Rastafarian groups seeking premises for club facilities – and had given them practical advice both on their planning and on possible sources of funding.

This had certainly done much to moderate their attitudes to police and policing. The group still resented police 'labelling' of Rastafarians – 'They call us all muggers, t'iefs, vagabonds, nobodies' – in much the same was as the young policemen resented the 'brutality' labelling of Rastafarians; but agreed that relationships had much improved, and that they were no longer subject to constant harassment by police on the streets. At the same time 'You have police and police.' Like Rastas in other groups, they made clear distinctions between the 'human' attitudes of the experienced beat officers and the 'authoritarian' approach of some young officers in the units.

Relationships of this kind are difficult to sustain. Rastafarian groups are themselves divided on so many issues: the extent to which they adhere to the tenets of the Rastafarian faith; use ganja; resort to criminality; accept economic dependence on 'Babylon'; or co-operate with the institutions of Babylon. Police contacts with a Rasta group, for example, may well breed deep suspicions in another; accusations of 'police grass-arse'; resentments; even threats of violence. Yet taken as a whole, the contacts that police have made with them during the period under review have at least established locally that police are 'talkable to', are a human presence rather than an ideological abstraction (it is so much harder to hate flesh and blood); and as officers such as David Webb and Martin Burton have shown, over time, their willingness to talk with groups on their terms, and often in their places, so a climate has been created in which the potential for conflict is gradually reduced, a potential for understanding and interchange slowly created.

This is not mere piety. The practical effects have ranged from Rastafarian participation in community events associated with the police, such as the Handsworth Festival (see pages 124–27) to Rastafarian contributions to local police training seminars for officers newly appointed to the subdivision. These sessions take place each quarter for a day and are designed to allow free exchanges between the newly appointed officers, local community leaders and spokesmen from other local services:

> 'The meeting with the Rastas was the most successful we've ever had. They were due to come for an hour, and they stayed for three. Both sides had a good old go at each other. It was a very healthy atmosphere. Police began to understand what it means to be a young unemployed black around here. The Rastas began to understand the problems of young coppers. And now, of course, they know each other as individuals: this bypasses the stereotyping on both sides.' (Chief Inspector Martin Burton)

The range and depth of contact between police and community in Handsworth has earned respect even from sources usually critical of police performance. 'Troubleshooter' of the *Caribbean Times*, for example, comments (15 May 1981) that:

> 'Webb has established . . . a network of community friendships second to none in England, thus ensuring regular and total feedback of community interests and anxieties. Contact and communication is clearly the basis of this police chief's thesis . . . Most of the immigrant leadership figure on Webb's network of projects and

committees, and he is no stranger to Indian weddings or functions and meetings all over his "patch". Doing a drink-about with Webb calls for the ability to walk fast and drink hard . . . This insistence on meeting and talking with every concernable organisation in Handsworth means that he can call on a community figure to call on noisy houseparties and so avoid unnecessary police presence at social gatherings . . . All in all, while Handsworth's MPs have been absent from the constituency's streets, it is Superintendent David Webb who has effectively been Handsworth's police chief, friend and MP.'

The reverse of this coin is engraved with the bitter criticisms of the very active political militants in the area, notably those in the Socialist Workers' Party and the Afro-Caribbean Self-Help Organisation. Floods of handbills and posters portray Webb's community-based approach to policing as nothing more than the old iron fist in a new velvet glove, a dangerously insidious form of social control; make capital out of every police error of judgement and suspect action, apparently in order to foment disaffection with police and to divide the community from them; and even, it also seems in some instances, to incite community groups to active confrontation and conflict.

Valid arguments stand out in this mass of propaganda, in particular those that point out the dangers of 'community policing' acting, or being used, as a mere palliative or cosmetic in a context of radical disadvantage, tackling symptoms, ignoring causes. But violent accusations predominant, the virulence of which is understandable. For those whose objectives are the breakdown of the present structures of society, community-based policing strategy is a far more formidable adversary than hard-line policing policies and practice, in that it undermines ideological stereotyping, and confronts extremist doctrines – and doctrinaire extremists – where they are least convincing and most vulnerable: on the middle ground.

Given the potential for communal disaffection and conflict in Handsworth, militant political groups have been conspicuously unsuccessful in translating this into communal action. Perhaps the best indicator of police effectiveness during the period under review has been the virtual absence of communal violence, despite public events with great potential for disorder, such as the Anti-Nazi League march referred to previously, and the African Liberation Day celebrations which took place in Handsworth 23–25 May 1981, to mark the 'Struggle for the Survival of the Black Race'.

Notable amongst indicators of growing trust and collaboration between police and community during the period under review have been the increasing willingness of local Asians and West Indians to volunteer for service with the Special Constabulary (by mid-1981, they represented well over half of some forty 'Specials' serving on the sub-division); and the increasing readiness of the community to come *to* the police as sources of help and advice on matters of personal and collective concern, and to consult with them on a wide range of community problems and activities. With community workers and politicos, suppliants and complainants, Ravidass and Rastamen, often mingling together in or around the offices of the Superintendent and his Deputy, and telephones ringing to bring more into the pipeline, Thornhill Road Police Station sometimes comes to resemble nothing so much as a community centre – or even, perhaps, the Town Hall.

Best evidence – and crowning symbol – of the nature and quality of police-community relations by the end of the period under review was provided by the Handsworth Festival of July 1981. This was the second of its kind, the first having taken place in the previous year, sponsored by the Handsworth Rotary Club following an initiative by David Webb amongst a number of community organisations. A wide range of community activities, ranging from national song and dance programmes to various sporting activities, were organised in Handsworth Park and attended by some two or three thousand people.

Despite its relative success, however, there were local criticisms that this was far too much of a 'police show'. The 1981 Festival was therefore organised on a much more extensive community basis, involving Handsworth Rotary and Round Table; the Faith and Confidence Fellowship Club; the Rialto Club, the West Indian Federation; the Guru Ravidass Association UK; the Birmingham Community Relations Council; the Midlands Community Growth Association; the Rangers and Continental Cricket Club; the Lozells Project; the Lucas Industries Tug-O-War Team; the Sikh Temple; the Federation of Indian Organisations; the Brotherhood of Justice Youth Council; and the West Midlands Police.

The Festival was a bright occasion in every respect against a dark national background, for the daily newspapers of 4 July 1981 reported clashes between skinheads and Asian youths in Southall, with several policemen injured as youths hurled stones and petrol bombs. Also reported was evidence to the Scarman Inquiry of police in Brixton singing to keep up their spirits behind their plastic riot shields. Then the morning radio spoke of conflict in Liverpool between police and skinheads. Violence on all sides, it seemed, was the order of the day.

But not in Handsworth Park that afternoon, where the sun shone bright on the young and old alike: blacks, whites, browns and blues, estimates of this great mix of people varying between eight and ten thousand.

Stalls and sideshows were organised by groups ranging from the Victims Support Scheme to Gee's Take-away (Mrs Edwards' delicious Jamaican patties and jerk pork); and the activities included a cricket knock-out competition; an open tug-o-war event (including county, national and European champions), a karate display, a dominoes knock-out competition, an eight-a-side football competition, a police mounted display and dog handling demonstration, wrestling, Asian and West Indian singing and dancing groups, the Handsworth Wood Girls School Gospel Choir, It's A (Multi-Racial) Knock-Out (expertly run by the Handsworth Fire Service), and reggae music and Afro-Caribbean cultural activities by a dozen Rastafarian groups.

The contribution of so many Rastafarian groups was all the more remarkable in view of the heavy pressures put upon them and others to boycott the festival by several, apparently linked, organisations, including the Socialist Workers Party and the Pan-African Congress Movement, who portrayed the event as 'A continuation of British colonial tactics in controlling African people . . . one cannot have funfair with one's jailers.'

Handbills littered the area like autumn leaves. 'Who is responsible for organising the so-called Handsworth Festival?', they asked. 'The clear answer is the police and their friends. What are their AIMS. (1) Total control. (2) To try to fool the world that black people are having a jolly nice time within the black communities of England when in reality those communities are just open prisons guarded by specially trained political police. WHO CAN THEY FOOL NOW? The Chairman of the Handsworth Festival is one of those police, divide and rule is their game, don't play.'

'Community policing' bore the brunt of the attack, being represented as a central means 'To beat down the resistance of the black community. . . First of all, Webb and Leivesley,* posing as students, go along to university, where they have access to all the information on the black community which is stored up in the books and computers in places like the Research Unit on Ethnic Relations at Aston University.'

Then, having attained money from the Inner Council partnership to create a community project, 'Policemen posing as social workers take black kids swimming and play football with them. They go into schools in Handsworth and give the children lectures on how nice the police really are. The police organise discos and run sound systems so people can dance away their frustrations. . . . But the people of Handsworth know that things are far from cool and calm. The police haven't stopped framing and beating up black people, the police haven't stopped ignoring racist attacks. . . BOYCOTT THE POLICE CARNIVAL.'

The success of this flood of propaganda could be measured in the park where there were certainly far more than a

---

* Superintendent Leivesley, head of the Public Liaison Department, West Midlands Police.

thousand Rastafarians amongst crowds of many races – a prospect guaranteed to ring alarm bells amongst proponents of 'overpolicing'. So how was the festival policed?

First, there were the five police officers on the organising committee – Superintendent Webb, Chief Inspector Burton, Sergeant Schuck, and PCs Charlie O'Donnell and Tim Green, all hard at work in casual dress – and they were supported by two uniformed PCs manning a police information vehicle. Patrolling of the park was undertaken by three permanent beat officers including a WPC, and four special constables, including a Sikh in an elegant blue-grey turban.

This represented the total police strength in and about the park during the whole course of the day, though various stewarding duties were also undertaken by other members of the festival committee; and the park gates seemed to be in the charge of a small West Indian with a big smile holding a notice pencilled on cardboard asking drivers to please go slow on driving away. 'Underpolicing', many senior policemen would certainly say. Yet it was plainly more than adequate for the occasion. No incidents of any kind were reported. No collars were felt. And accusations of police 'appeasement' would be quite beside the point. A group with me wandered about all afternoon, four or five hours together, and none of us saw the slightest signs of tension, let alone conflict, except when the tug of war teams were in action (the Punjabi Farmers soon putting paid to the West Midlands Police), or the slightest sign of violence, except what brown-skinned 'goodies' like Sucha Singh were doing to white-skinned 'baddies' in the wrestling ring.

People of all races moved freely at ease, stopping to watch the entertainments or just to sprawl on the grass, to take the sun, while the kids rushed off to the ice cream van. Brummies in shirt sleeves rubbed shoulders with girls in ethnic dresses, Sikh elders with long, white beards, young Rastas in sharp gear. And there in the midst of all, an old English couple selecting their spot to sit, spreading a cloth on the grass, laying out their picnic with care, eating in peace: key symbols of personal security – the acid test of it all.

The ambiguities of Handsworth crowded in again that same evening, however, when events made plain how tender is the plant of peace there, how exposed it is to ill winds from political, economic and racial quarters. Some three hundred representatives of community groups had come together in the assembly rooms of a local pub to celebrate the success of the Festival, and after drinks and a well-flavoured curry, prizes were presented and speeches made by community leaders. All stressed their pride in what had been created in Handsworth, the unity of their resolve to live in multi-racial peace; and the Asian leaders, with skinhead attacks in Southall fresh in their minds, put particular emphasis on the need to guard against outsiders who might seek to subvert or destroy their hard-won harmony.

This was a cue for heckling by a small group of political activists who had been allowed entry. In a spirit of tolerance, they were permitted to put their views to the audience, and a black man and girl made vehement attacks on the festival as a betrayal of the black community to white racist society and on the police as racist oppressors of black people. Two white activists, apparently their armourers, nodded in tune. A number of participants drifted away. David Webb, as the elected Chairman of the Festival Committee, stood quietly by. Their speeches concluded, the activists made to leave, but were challenged by a number of Rastafarian young men and women at the door and finally ejected by them, the very people they were most concerned to incite and inflame.

A further flood of militant handbills followed hard on the heels of the Festival, with calls to picket the 'notorious torture centre' which is Thornhill Road Police Station, 'a world-wide model for community policing in beating down black resistance to oppression'. The intentions of this propaganda were clearly to divide the community from the police, and to attack and discredit the police leader who had done so much to create effective alliance between them. One activist was quite open about this. 'If we get rid of Webb, we can have this place.' The reasoning was that if they could undermine the credibility of the police leader primarily responsible for shaping this model

– for police and society – of police-community contact in this key test area, they could also do much to discredit the policing philosophy with which he is identified.

Thus despite celebrations of the festival – 'This one community show', as an Indian businessman described it – and the resolve for unity amongst community leaders, there was no doubt that the peace of Handsworth was to prove precarious.

How precarious I learnt a week after the festival, as news came of riots in Handsworth on the night of Friday, 10 July. Returning there to talk with eye-witnesses, I found their reactions confirmed at a public meeting called by local shopkeepers on the evening of Wednesday, 15 July, also attended by community leaders, local Labour and Conservative councillors, and Superintendent Webb. Most of those present had had direct experience of the rioting.

A clear pattern of events emerged from their diverse perspectives. After the festival, activist meetings had led to the picketing of Thornhill Road Police Station. Tensions grew against a background of violence in other major cities of Britain. Local West Indian, Asian and other community leaders therefore met together on Thursday, 9 July at the Shri Guru Ravidass Cultural Association, and issued a 'Resolution' expressing their concern

> 'about the troubles and violence which have been taking place and escalating in the major cities of this country during the past week. The causes and reasons for this violence and disorder are many and varied. In many instances we feel that the criticisms of police action to contain the situation are justified and that more could have been done to prevent trouble before it started or to contain it once it began.
>
> The majority of leaders and representatives of the Handsworth community support the initiatives and work of the police in our area, but urge them not to be complacent and to continue to listen and be accountable to the community and to behave in such a way as to retain the respect and support of those they are paid to serve.

We urge all our people to behave in a responsible way and not to take the law into their own hands. Let us live in Peace and Harmony.'

Several of those responsible for this 'Resolution', notably some Asian leaders, are also officials of national political and religious organisations – the Indian Congress Party UK, the Guru Ravidass Association UK, etc. Handsworth's community networks therefore have close connections with those in other parts of the country, notably Southall.

On the morning of Friday, 10 July, rumours that there would be a Skinhead/National Front march on the Soho Road against coloured people that evening were very successfully spread throughout the area by radio and by word of mouth. Police did their best to scotch these rumours, but groups of apprehensive people gathered that evening on the Soho Road. Superintendent Webb and other officers walked up and down the road, attempting to calm their fears.

Eye witnesses at the public meeting identified a mixed group of white, Asian and West Indian youths hanging around at that time with a group of activists, allegedly from the Socialist Workers Party. Just before 10 p.m., reports of a riot on the Soho Road were put out on CB radio. At 10 p.m., Superintendent Webb was challenged and attacked by the group of youths. There were chants of 'Get Webb'. He was struck on the head by two bricks, kicked and punched, but was rescued from further attack by Asians and West Indians standing by.

As he was taken to the police station, rioting immediately broke out. Eye witnesses claimed that the youths responsible were armed for smashing windows and looting. Some twenty to twenty-five shops suffered damage, six or seven to a serious extent. Notably, very few Rastafarians were involved. Indeed, one eye witness account in a local newspaper (*Birmingham Evening Mail*, Wednesday, 15 July 1981) spoke of Rastafarians attempting to damp down the violence:

'a group of young Rastafarians vehemently pointed out to an excited group of young people that they were being agitated by white political extremists who had no interest in the well-being of Handsworth. The Rastafarians told the crowd that the agitators had lied about there being an imminent attack by skinheads. The group respected the feelings of the Rastafarians and the gathering broke up. I saw a West Indian peacefully disarm an excited young man of a brick. I heard a European pleading with Handsworth people to end the violence.'*

Local officers did what they could to stem the rioting. Amongst them was Sergeant Schuck:

'We had the first news of the violence, and of activists at the centre of things, when Mr Webb came back injured. We went down in the van, and were being very badly stoned. I think the police officers were shook up quite a bit. We were very very few in number, but had no alternative but to charge the rioters. We numbered about fifteen, and two sergeants, and of course at my age, I'm not a great deal of use anyhow. But they were very brave when they went to break up a crowd of about one hundred and fifty. It made me immensely proud of the police force, of a spirit that must never be chipped away. Then reinforcements arrived. The looting was gradually quelled. The great thing was that within two hours of us gaining control of the situation, we were able to establish our traditional rapport with the people, and police officers were openly talking to groups of black and brown and white youths on the streets.'

On the next evening, there was another, less successful, attempt at looting on the Lozells Road. This was quickly put down by a strong police response. After that, things went quiet again.

At the shopkeepers' meeting, there was general agreement that the community had been manipulated, and that those responsible must be found and excluded from the area.

---

* H.G. Taylor, Beeches Road, Great Barr.

Community trust in, and support for, the police was strongly endorsed; and ways suggested to reinforce interchange and links between police and community groups.

All political and racial shades joined in rejecting the road to water-cannon, CS gas, and the many suggestions for a 'tin' blue line then being bruited by police and politicos through the media; reasserted their resolve to defend the peace and racial harmony of Handsworth; and reaffirmed their belief that this could best be achieved through a strategy of community policing.

Ted Schuck summed up on much the same lines:

> 'I think that the last three and a half years have given me a chance to look back at the police service, and perhaps reassess its place in society. If I had any doubts about the new ideas I'd gained during that time, they were dispersed by the experience on the Friday night of the riots in Handsworth. I saw then that those ideas were right. Without the backing of the general public in Handsworth we would not have had the flexibility to put down the riots firmly and decisively and then to immediately revert back to friendly relations with the community. Some policemen think you can't do both. We were able to do both. That's what "policing by consent" means.'

Three months later, in October 1981, Superintendent Webb decided to retire early from the police service, believing that there was insufficient support for a community-based approach to policing within police ranks, and a lack of will at some senior levels to translate it into operational reality.

Community responses to this decision ranged from 'sad' and 'dismaying' to 'understandable' and 'inevitable'. Police responses were far more ambiguous, ranging from 'regrettable' to 'good riddance', so that even in the manner of his going, Webb exposed both the divisions within the service towards the policing policies he had advocated and enacted, and the divisions between police and public in their expectations and assessments of police work. A reconciling note was struck, however, with the announcement of Martin Burton's appointment as sub-divisional commander in succession to David Webb. Community groups took this as an earnest of continuity in local policing policy and practice.

10 *Assessments*

How should or can we assess police performance? Thinking on this score is both confused and divided. The common use of criminal statistics as central reference points suggests that many (police and others) still see 'law enforcement' as the essential frame for assessment. But this is to confuse means with ends. Quite apart from the fact that it rarely constitutes more than a quarter of police business, even in the highest crime areas, law enforcement is only one of many means that police employ to serve the ends for which society created them: to protect life and property; to preserve the public tranquility; and to prevent and detect crime. Equally, police are only one of many services and forces in society which contribute to those ends.

Given the inherent nature of policing – as a process of *interaction* between police and society; the divisions between police and public perspectives on that process; the perpetually changing and varying nature of its social contexts; its vulnerability to the caprices of local, national and international policies and circumstances; the limited validity of all relevant sources of data; and not least, the severe limitations of most available tools of measurement – the tasks of assessing police performance are, to say the least, daunting. It is certainly useful to associate whatever (partially) relevant data are available from quantitative and qualitative sources with whatever (partially) relevant evidence is available from public and police perspectives. The more sources of data and the more human perspectives that can be brought to bear on police performance, the more valid assessments are likely to be, though by their nature they will be, at best, approximate.

Since assessments of police performance must also, of necessity, be set in comparative frames of reference, i.e. related to past police performance in the same areas, or to contemporary performance in areas with similar communities and characteristics, problems of assessment multiply. So many – often radical – changes of context, ranging from unemployment pressures to population shifts. So few constants, so many variables.

Thus this study cannot claim to do more than offer a rough chart of police performance in Handsworth. As such, it cannot indicate precise routes for police policy and practice in comparable areas, though it may at least be able to suggest useful general directions.

Amidst doubts on routes to assessment, and all the ambiguities of the Handsworth scene, one issue stands clear: that both in the absolute terms of police purposes in society, and in the comparative terms of policing in areas with similar characteristics, the key police achievement in Handsworth has been its capability to realise the central police objective – to keep the peace – with the backing and active support of the great majority of local people in a context of growing, and extremely adverse, social/economic and militant political pressures.

In terms of the protection of life and property, the account is more complex. On the profit side, major items include: more police about on the streets, and more people about on the streets; a decrease in crimes of violence against people and property on the streets, and an increase in public perceptions of their own security, individual and collective. But are those items related, and if so, in what ways? In particular, what is the nature and extent of the interaction, if any, between the development of police-community contact in Handsworth, and the development of the area as a thriving commercial centre during the period under review? Thus however clearly marked individual items of 'profit' may be, the issues underlying them are just as clearly open to debate. Not so with recorded items of 'loss', where the outstanding entry is the increase in burglaries of local dwelling houses, though this trend is roughly in line with national and European trends in major urban areas.

Issues relating to the prevention and detection of crime are rather more clear-cut. Apart from their usefulness as a deterrent presence on the streets, the preventive networks that local PBOs have created on their beats with neighbourhood associations, teachers and parents, community, youth and social workers, as well as through activities associated with the Lozells Project, have done much to reinforce (as they are reinforced by) the work of the sub-divisional commander and his deputy in defusing, damping down, heading off or simply allaying potential sources of local conflict. Though gradual, long term and unamenable to precise measurement, their preventive effects are already as widespread as they are widely acknowledged.

Yet there is little or no evidence to suggest that increased community contact has meant greater flows of criminal intelligence from public to police, and thus better detection rates. Clear-up rates for main categories of crime – burglary, in particular – have remained 'shamefully low' during the period under review. This does not mean that the evidence of Handsworth in this sphere can be used as a valid basis for generalisation, however. It contrasts sharply with the evidence of the Skelmersdale policing experiment, for example, in which radical improvements in clear-up rates for burglary (from 31.9 per cent in 1978 to 56.8 per cent in 1980) could be specifically related to improved community contact by small local area teams of foot patrol officers.[9]

So are there key differences of police experience between the two areas? Two stand out, I suggest: that in Skelmersdale, the functions of local beat officers and those of the local CID have been more closely associated or co-ordinated; and that hard-core offenders there have been far more willing to co-operate with police investigations after arrest. The organisation of 'grass-root' police community contact on a *team* rather than on an individual officer basis has almost certainly also made a positive contribution to detection success in Skelmersdale.

Surveyed as a whole, however, the community-based approach to policing developed in Handsworth over recent years represents, by any comparative standards, a notable model of 'policing by consent' in a multi-racial urban context, admirably balancing the two key elements of 'effectiveness' and 'acceptability'. Recognition of this achievement became widespread after the 1981 riots in Brixton and other comparable areas: summer and autumn 1981 saw a constant procession of visitors to Thornhill Road Police Station, ranging from civic groups from other riot areas of Britain to senior European policemen, from media men to Lord Scarman. This attention evoked – to my certain knowledge – a measure of jealousy and resentment amongst the police tribe, both locally and nationally, so that public praise was often counter-pointed by private police criticism. The nub of that criticism was that the Handsworth policing model depended far too much upon the 'one off' personality of the sub-divisional commander and far too little upon *structural* improvements in police organisation.

Both these critical points demand closer analysis, for both have a certain validity. During the period under review, policing in Handsworth was certainly dominated by David Webb's personality and his concepts of the police role in society. Recognising that the quality of policing depends upon the quality of police community inter-action, he led by example: he identified himself with the needs of the area and its people, immersed himself in local affairs at many and various levels, and by virtue of personal commitment and a willingness to make himself freely and widely available and accountable to local people, made himself a central reference point for community thinking and action. In consequence, public respect for, trust in, and co-operation with, police, was greatly enhanced and improved at local level during a time, and in a context, of national anxiety, doubt and debate on policing strategy.

Yet it is imperative to recognise that this collaborative model of policing also derived from the philosophy and leadership of the Chief Constable, Sir Philip Knights, and was the achievement not of one, but of many officers working at many levels with other agencies and with community groups. Some of the initiatives they have developed have become self-sustaining, and during the time of writing of this study (summer 1981 to spring 1982) it has become increasingly apparent that – given a continuing commitment to the same principles of policing – these initiatives are likely both to continue and to develop in their own right after Webb's retirement from the West Midlands Force.

A more telling criticism is that just as Webb's 'consensus' policing policy in Handsworth in some measure served to mask deficiencies in public policies as a whole in the area, so his personal initiatives in some measure also served to mask central weaknesses in the policing *system*: divisions of purpose; inflexibility in organisational structures; inadequacies in training programmes. But it is scarcely pertinent to criticise the local sub-divisional commander on this score, since the sources of these weaknesses are located at national rather than at local policy levels.

Ironically, these weaknesses may to some extent be associated with drives for greater professional efficiency within the police service during the 1960s and 1970s. 'Professionalism' is a prized and vaunted concept within the police service, but as enacted in recent years it abounds with ambiguities. In Britain, its main directions have been organisation and technical: these have been given practical expression in terms of force amalgamations, more and more specialist units, major shifts from foot to vehicle patrolling, more sophisticated information and communication systems, more effective weaponry, etc.

But the experience of policing the riots in major cities of Britain in 1981 confirms that greater police efficiency in these terms has not meant greater public effectiveness. Indeed, the one may well have worked *against* the other in several notable and related ways. Firstly, large-scale police bureaucracies have been created at the expense of local patterns of policing: centralising trends in organisation and decision-making, reinforced by command and control computer systems, have tended both to diminish police reponsibility and accountability at local levels, and to impair the capability of local commanders to deploy their resources in ways most flexible and responsive to local needs. (Whether the standard 3 × 8 hour equal shift system represents the most effective deployment of manpower resources in Handsworth or anywhere else is, to say the least, debatable.)

Sir Philip Knights, Chief Constable of the West Midlands Police, gave recognition to problems inherent in these trends in a perceptive article in the *Police Journal* of October 1981.[10] His force area comprehends seven metropolitan districts (Birmingham, Coventry, Dudley, Sandwell, Solihull, Walsall and Wolverhampton) with a current population of 2,696,000.

'Therein lie the roots of the biggest of our problems. Given such a concentration of population, divided into seven, almost totally autonomous authorities, how does one organise and maintain the local contacts undoubtedly fundamental to effective policing? With seven education authorities, seven social service departments, seven housing departments, six (only) community relations councils, how can one satisfactorily develop common policies in fields such as juvenile delinquency or community relations? There must be grounds for debate whether the county council, with 104 elected representatives, let alone the police authority with 16 elected representatives and 8 magistrates, can really claim to voice the wishes of the community at large in policing affairs.

Personally, I feel that as a police area it is too big and that the police force, unless one works very hard at it, can become very remote and impersonal. . . Certainly I would not wish to see any forces created larger than we now have them – the reverse if possible.'

Sir Philip's observations evoked a refreshingly direct response by Sir Ranulph Bacon in the following issue of the *Police Journal*. 'So to Sir Philip's headache – that of policing with acceptance one of the six metropolitan districts outside London. To use blunt language, all of them are just too damn big.'[11] That hits the nail on the head. It is hardly a coincidence that the British police force with the most centralised bureaucratic structures and the most complex lines of communication – the Metropolitan police – appears at the time of writing to have the greatest problems in organising and maintaining 'the local contacts undoubtedly fundamental to effective policing'.

But what scale of police organisation can best serve these ends? If, as the evidence in Handsworth very strongly suggests, the sub-division is an appropriate scale on which to create an *operationally* effective network of local contacts,* this points to the value of de-centralising police organisation and evolving police decision-making in ways which can best encourage the development of local 'patch' systems of local crime control. Concepts of this kind, and practices on these lines, are already developing in the spheres of medical and social work, for very similar reasons;[12] and the 1980s are likely to reveal ever stronger professional, economic and political imperatives to create 'patch' systems of care and order across the whole spectrum of social policy and practice, linking professional effectiveness to public accountability.

It is within this general context that police will have to review their own policies and organisation, balancing needs for greater decentralisation to combat local 'mass' crime (theft; burglary; street robbery; criminal damage, etc.) against needs for greater centralisation to combat the crime and disorder which have national or international bases (terrorism, fraud and currency offences, drugs, art and antiques theft, and other 'professional' areas of criminality).

---

* In terms of manpower, the Handsworth sub-division (some 250 officers) is roughly in line with the average size of police *forces* in Holland and Denmark.

Centralisation versus decentralisation issues must also be associated with issues of specialist versus generalist functions within the police service. Here again, considerations of professional efficiency at times find themselves at odds with those of public effectiveness: the successes of the increasing number of specialist units designed to cope with new, or developing, forms of crime and disorder must certainly be measured against their negative effects. Of central concern are the ways in which specialist functions have come to take growing precedence, and assume growing status, over generalist patrol functions. These have led to a progressive devaluation of the traditional police role 'on the ground'. Aspiring officers have come to measure 'success' by the speed with which they get off the streets and into specialist units: the streets have too largely and too often been left to green lads and uniform carriers, to growing dismay – and mounting criticism – amongst the general public; and the very base of police effectiveness and acceptability in the eyes of that public – the quality of operational contact – has thus been dangerously eroded. In brief, traditional police ideology ('the most important man is the man on the beat') and contemporary police organisation have come to seem not merely at variance, but in head-on conflict.

Of related concern are the ways in which the creation of more and more specialist units, some seemingly intent on doing their own thing in their own way, has also served to obstruct the development of coherent strategies and co-ordinated tactics. Just as centralisation stratifies police organisation from top to bottom, so specialisation stratifies it from side to side. Fragmented and inconsistent policies and practice may result, which at times not only disconcert, dismay or antagonise the public, but also spark dangerous tensions within the police service.

Classic reference points have been provided over the last decade by Special Patrol Group stop and search operations in multi-racial inner city areas. After one such operation in Brixton in 1973, for example, designed to combat the growing incidence of street robberies and thefts, mainly committed by young West Indians, the SPG commander claimed it as an effective method of crime control; local CID officers claimed it did no more than cause a temporary displacement of crime (a view reinforced by officers of adjoining police divisions); and local home beat officers claimed it as 'a bloody disaster'. ('What's the good of short-term "solutions" that cause long-term problems of fouled-up working relationships?') Reactions among local people ranged from mild concern to bitter hostility and public demonstrations against the Metropolitan police. Some even claimed that the main effect of the operation would be to fuel aggravation and violence amongst West Indian youth.[13] Evidence submitted to Lord Scarman's Inquiry into the Brixton Disorders in 1981 suggested that perspectives on policing in the area were still as disparate eight years later.

Though perspectives on policing are far less disparate in Handsworth, they remain uneasily divergent between different arms of the police service, and are likely to continue so until CID and other specialist functions are more firmly integrated into local strategies. Even more fundamental are the problems relating to the status of uniform officers responsible for local 'contact' policing. Given that quality of policing depends primarily upon quality of police-community interaction, police must certainly give greater priority and recognition to contact functions, not only through their commendation and promotion systems, but also by offering better incentives and career prospects for good policemen to stay on the ground as neighbourhood or area officers in order to develop those sustained relationships which alone can generate effective interaction between police and community. To achieve this end, it may well be necessary to create new *lateral* promotion structures within the police service, as has been successfully achieved by the West Berlin police (see Appendix B).

Problems in this sphere relate to those which derive from increasing reliance upon reactive or 'fire-brigade' styles of policing over recent years, emphasising speed rather than quality of police response, at the expense of the preventive functions defined by the first Commissioner in 1829 as 'the primary object of an efficient police'. (Amongst all too many within the police culture, 'prevention' has been relegated to marginal status – merely a matter of 'locks, bolts and bars'.) This trend goes hand in hand with growing emphasis upon the enforcement role of the police at the expense of the service role. The line of reasoning here is that as demands upon police intensify, the greater priority they must give to their 'first duty' – as many policement call it – to enforce the law. ('Service to the community? That's for wankers.')

This is a standard 'no bloody nonsense practical copper' stance. It is very far from being practical. Not only does it confuse means with ends, but it fails to recognise that it is precisely the essential *duality* of the police role – enforcement *and* service – which is the true source both of police effectiveness and of police acceptability, effectiveness and acceptability being themselves *interdependent* in traditions of 'policing by consent'. It fails to recognise, in fact, what the Handsworth experience amply confirms – that the very nature of 'policing by consent' is a continuous process of interaction and reciprocation, or as some would say, a form of social contract, negotiated, and constantly renegotiated, between the two active elements of police and society.

The Handsworth experience also confirms awareness amongst both public and police of deficiencies in the training of police officers for this dual role. Whilst there are necessary emphases on police powers, and on practical methods to enact them, during police training, there are inadequate emphases on the ways in which police roles and responsibilities should and could relate to those of other professional (and voluntary) services concerned with care and order in society. Thus young police officers often appear as ignorant of the roles and responsibilities of employment, housing, youth, education, probation and social services, as young practitioners in those spheres often appear to be about police roles and responsibilities. In consequence, mutual ignorance often vies uneasily with awareness of needs to work collaboratively at practitioner level, much as at command and police level that awareness vies uneasily with tribal fears of compromising professional independence.

In the article previously referred to, Sir Philip Knights goes on to suggest that 'it is essential to work as a team with local authority professions, and this has implications for training. Why not joint courses at Bramshill?' But given the strength and the ambiguities of professionalism in the public services, divided both between and amongst themselves on issues of working 'as a team', joint courses at Bramshill would scarcely suffice – even if a uniformed environment were appropriate – to overcome tribal insularities.

To reduce such insularities to manageable levels, and to create a climate for greater collaboration, would certainly require a programme at once more structured and more comprehensive. For the police, this might include:

1 Increasing opportunities for police at all levels – *not least during initial training* – to share the experience of other agencies and of community groups in non-conflict circumstances, so that they can relate their professional functions more effectively and acceptably to them at both policy and practitioner level.
2 Creating joint consultative structures with other agencies at command level to co-ordinate policy directions; develop new models of collaborative practice; and initiate research studies on common problems.
3 Linked to (2) – encouraging joint 'problem-centred' sessions at 'patch' levels between local statutory, voluntary and community groups to develop collaborative thinking and action in tune with local needs.
4 Helping to set up combined training courses for professional groups (ranging from planning, employment and housing to education and social services) at junior and senior command levels, with emphasis on themes relating to the interdependence of professional policy and practice in the public services, and on studies of working models of collaborative policy and practice in various environments. (These working models could thus be used as test-beds for policy change.)

In the wake of the 1981 riots, one issue, at least appears to command a measure of agreement within the police service at the time of writing: the need for changes in police training designed – in Lord Scarman's words – 'to develop the understanding that good community relations are not merely necessary but essential to good policing . . . the central theme of all training must be the need for the police to secure the consent and support of the public if they are successfully to perform their duties'.[14] Yet changes in training on these lines will not have full meaning to trainees – or indeed, very much meaning at all – if commitment to a community-based approach to policing is not fully endorsed at force policy levels, or not fully enacted at divisional and sub-divisional command levels, or if specialist arms of the police service keep doing these things explicitly at odds with that approach, or if the canteen culture – arguably the most important formative influence on the service – keeps on saying things explicitly at odds with that approach.

And therein lie the rubs. The pre- and post-Scarman debate has exposed divisions rather than unity of purpose within the police service; embattled or aggressive postures rather than critical revaluations of strategy; policies and personalities at odds with each other; and from the Association of Chief Police Officers a dismaying failure to give a lead in defining common objectives and priorities for the service. All of which is likely to inspire more voices to make chief constables more accountable to society.

During the time of writing of this study, this disunity has become increasingly apparent, and is clearly rooted in very disparate perspectives on policing and police strategy. On the one hand is the perspective which insists that 'policing is for the police', and which continues to see 'solutions' to crime and disorder mainly in terms of more professional resources and more purposeful police policies. On the other hand is the perspective which insists that professional resources cannot themselves be more than marginal to the control of crime and disorder; and that since the primary resources for control lie within society, police must seek to work with and through society as fully and effectively as possible, and to link their policies to public policies in this sphere.

From these perspectives derive very different attitudes on relationships between police and communities. The first understandably views good community relations as essentially marginal to 'real policing', primarily 'a public relations exercise' 'to show the flag' and 'to keep the public sweet' and 'on our side'. The second views good community relations as the very essence, 'the life blood', of effective – and acceptable – policing.

The evidence of Handsworth implicitly challenges the first perspective, and explicitly validates the second. It demonstrates that police effectiveness cannot be dissociated from 'good community relations', since each depends primarily on the quality of *operational* contact between police and public. And it suggests that both public satisfaction and public willingness to co-operate with police are closely related to the ways in which local officers show themselves responsible and accountable in their everyday contacts at grass-root level.

'Community relations' are thus not a matter to be left to specialist police liaison departments. This is not to deny that such departments can be helpful in supporting or facilitating police-community interaction at operational levels; but the more they are seen as marginal to police operations, the less credible they will be within the service; and the more they are seen as a public relations cover for failures in operational contact between police and community, the less credible they will be to the public at large.

On the issue of liaison, the Handsworth experience very strongly suggests that where the public are assured of police responsibility and accountability at operational – or *primary* – levels, and where a multiplicity of effective voluntary links has been created between police and public throughout the community, pressures to assure police responsibility and accountability through formal – or *secondary* – systems of liaison are minimal. If the reverse is true – as recent experience in other key urban areas also suggests – the implications for the police service are very plain. Pressures for formal liaison systems are likely to be strongest where police community liaison at operational levels is weakest. And if formal liaison systems prove inadequate to reconcile police effectiveness with public acceptability, whether through police intransigence or political ill-will or mixtures of both, then pressures for a *tertiary* system, involving forms of public *control* of police, may well prove irresistible. The preservation of an independent policing tradition thus crucially depends on the extent to which chief officers of police are willing to give real – as distinct from rhetorical – priority to the creation of community-based systems of policing responsive to local circumstances and needs.

Police experience in Handsworth, like that of the Devon and Cornwall Prevention Unit in Exeter,[15] also suggests that a community-based approach to policing sets in motion invaluable processes of reciprocation between police and public. The more police involve themselves in the community, the more people in the community are willing to involve themselves with the police, and to join in co-operative efforts to keep their locale secure against crime and disorder. And the more that they become involved in such efforts, the greater their understanding of, and support for, police and police objectives. These processes are exemplified at many levels in Handsworth, ranging from neighbourhood associations to shopkeepers' organisations, but perhaps nowhere better than in the ways that volunteers from local ethnic minority groups have come forward before and after the riots to join the Special Constabulary. In the comparative context of other urban areas affected by the riots, this is a remarkable achievement, and the pity is that police professionalism continues to restrict the potential of the Special Constabulary as a key auxiliary force to protect life and property, to keep the peace and to control crime.

Similar processes of reciprocation derive from collaborative strategies between police and other public services; and the Handsworth experience suggests that these are most effective when focused on common problems at local or 'patch' levels. Yet as the Lozells Project shows, the benefits of collaboration come hand in hand with inherent problems.

Few would deny either the originality or the usefulness of the Lozells Project as an initiative in inter-agency collaboration. But though it is still too early to attempt any overall assessment of its impact, two problem areas can be readily identified. The first is that of the respective roles and relationships of the various services involved. Because police initiative – primarily that of Sir Philip Knights – was the main motive force which brought the project into being, it was understandable that police should make the running in setting up its organisation. It was equally understandable that, as at the formation of the Exeter Policing Consultative Committee, local authority services were in favour of the police, as the only service independent of local authority, taking the chair. But with the financial accounts of the project in police hands, and with police commitment of manpower to the project so dominant, doubts multiplied, particularly within the probation and social services, as to whether the Lozells Project was a genuinely co-operative or a police-led venture.

Both from the Handsworth and Exeter experience, it appears that whilst local statutory and voluntary groups are willing to accept police in the roles of initiators, catalysts or collaborators in new projects, they are considerably resistant to accepting police in a leadership role. More grass-root consultation, a more communal approach to decision-making and a greater sharing of responsibilities would almost certainly have evoked greater support for, and commitment to, the Lozells Project during its formative stages – though police can hardly take the blame on this score since Sir Philip Knights had originally tried to induce the local authority to take on leadership of the project, only to meet a unanimous vote for police leadership. In the event, it is fortunate that police willingness to learn from experience, and to adopt a more flexible, co-operative approach seems – at the time of writing – to be overcoming community resistance to the project, and to be commanding greater local backing and involvement.

The second problem area concerns the *limits* of the Lozells Project. Whilst it has made valuable contributions to social and educational facilities in the area, the limited nature of its collaborative network has so far prevented it making any significant contribution in the sphere of youth training and employment. In a context of rising unemployment, this sphere had rapidly become of key local concern, and if the Lozells Project is to have a central place in the life of the area, its most useful contribution could well be through collaborative projects aimed at improving local youth skills and employment opportunities.

Whilst youth unemployment and youth crime in Handsworth cannot be specifically correlated, most local crime is committed by young people under the age of 25, many of them unemployed; and since rising youth unemployment increases the numbers of dissatisfied young people with unchannelled energies, it can only increase *potential* for criminality. All the statistical evidence indicates that this potential is lowest in Handsworth amongst youth of Asian birth or descent; higher amongst British youth; and highest amongst youth of West Indian birth or descent.

But any attempt to make a simple correlation between West Indian youth crime and frustrations born of unemployment would be a crass distortion of local realities. My own experience very strongly suggests that the West Indian offender most typical of Handsworth has a number of salient characteristics. At the time of writing, he is likely not only to be unemployed or irregularly employed, but also Jamaican by birth, raised by female relatives until shipped to this country to join his parents, and with divided schooling, weak educational skills and a dislocated family background. Indeed, he may well have either rejected, or been rejected by, his family group, and be seeking solace, purpose and identity within the Rastafarian subculture, leading with others of his kind a mainly communal, hand-to-mouth 'survival' way of life in which distinctions between 'legal' and 'illegal' have lost a good deal of meaning.

The complexity of pressures that have shaped these characteristics cannot be confined to those within British society. Many derive from a Caribbean cultural inheritance. In Jamaica some twenty years ago, V.S. Naipaul noted that 'Rastas have developed their own psychology of survival. They reply to rejection with rejection. . . Many will not work, turning necessity into principle; and many console themselves with marijuana, which God himself smokes.' The movement derived, he perceived, from the pressures of Jamaican society, and 'the pressures in Jamaica were not simply the pressures of race or those of poverty. They were the accumulated pressures of the slave society, the colonial society, the under-developed, over-populated agricultural country. The situation required a society which understood itself and had purpose and direction. . .'[16]

Lacking a base of strong family and community structures, relationships and values; rejecting on the one hand the Jamaican inheritance as embodied by their own families, and on the other, the British inheritance, as embodied by what appear as oppressive and discriminatory institutions; and seeking refuge in the powerful myth – sanctified by religious faith – of an African inheritance, the Rasta youth inherits a 'limbo' world, where individuality vies with group conformity, insecurity with aggression, creative instincts with attitudes of negation. And as external pressures grow, so more and more young people of West Indian descent take cover within its ideology and its 'survival' ways of life, lock themselves into them, and sustain themselves there.

So what forms of policing are most appropriate to respond to groups of this kind in environments such as Handsworth? Experience there suggests that they will certainly need to focus on causes as well as symptoms of disaffection and criminality. This means preventive as well as reactive responses by the police, though these are not likely to be very effective unless clearly related and co-ordinated.

At the primary level of law enforcement action, police responses seem most likely to be effective when closely targeted on hard-core criminal offenders, when undertaken by local officers who know their targets and the ground, and when supported by local people. This last condition may not be as unlikely as many policemen think. As Pat Murphy observes in *Commissioner* – a work of most uncommon good sense on policing – most people, black, white or brown, are 'not only law-abiding, but also possibly law-assisting'. The police job, he suggests, 'is to enlist the law-abiding allies in the struggle against crime and criminals': and in many inner city environments, personal insecurity is now becoming a powerful motive for communal action.

Yet police are unlikely to harness public co-operation if they cannot convince the public that police action is specifically related to public needs. And they are most likely to do so if they work in close and sustained contact with community groups at local levels, keep them fully informed of police purposes (including the reasons for, and limits of, those purposes), and where possible, let local people share in defining them. The more police act in isolation, and have recourse to insensitive and indiscriminate tactics, the more likely they are to do more harm than good in public eyes, and thus to forfeit the public acceptance and assistance which are essential for effective policing.

Local people are also more likely to back law enforcement action where they see this go hand in hand with vigorous preventive action, and most of all, when they themselves have a hand in that preventive action. At this second level of response, police seem likely to be most effective in their preventive functions when they take on catalytic and collaborative roles, working on a partnership basis with other agencies and community organisations to protect life and property and to keep the peace. But Handsworth suggests that this is not likely to be achieved unless police commanders accept that they have a prime responsibility to create effective *structures* of collaboration for their officers to work in; are prepared to give priority to community contact functions; and are willing to devolve responsibility to suitably trained and experienced officers, or groups of officers, to work with other statutory and voluntary groups in local 'patch' systems of care and order.

Of prime concern to work of this kind are the youth at risk, black, white or brown, on the fringes of criminality, and Handsworth points to the value, as well as the problems, of winning their trust and confidence, associating with their activities and attempting to work with and through them. This suggests a third level of response, at which police work with other professional and voluntary services to assist disadvantaged groups to develop their own 'self-help' activities, whether in social/cultural/recreational terms or – as increasingly dictated by the pressures of youth unemployment – in terms of skills training and employment opportunities.

Those who would argue that this is not a police role will find it difficult to deny that it can have much to do with keeping the peace, particularly in areas of high unemployment. The peace of Handsworth, for example, may well be greatly influenced by whether or not Rasta-style groups are able to demonstrate their worth in their own eyes, and in the eyes of society, through 'self-help' activities. On this score, the ambiguities run deep. There is evidence of the need, the will and the skills to develop such activities amongst some Rasta groups. There is also evidence that conflicting currents of motive and consciousness within these groups put their capability in doubt: impulses to achieve in society's terms at odds with impulses to reject those terms, reinforced by the tempting lures of 'survival' ways of life.

Issues here are as complex as they are crucial to the peace of the area, and in such a context, remedies are desperately difficult to define. Yet the evidence of Handsworth does – tentatively at least – suggest the value – if not the necessity – of purposeful, carefully monitored, step-by-step programmes of investment in selected 'self-help' groups to assist them in developing the training, practical and marketing skills they need to mount co-operative projects and business ventures. It also suggests the ways in which police can usefully assist and facilitate developments on these lines, and the value of assuming this role.

This role points to a fourth level of police response – that of advising on aspects of public policy which bear upon police functions. Again, there are some both within and outside the police service who would cavil at this. But given that policing functions in a complex interplay of forces – political, legal, economic, social and cultural – the nature of which does much to determine the problems which police have to face (in Handsworth the outstanding examples are those involving Rasta-style youth), it would surely be as unwise to deny police this right as it would be to deny the public the right to advise on those aspects of policing policy which bear upon their vital interests.

In sum, the Handsworth experience points the value of a policing strategy which comprehends functions ranging from enforcing the law, through participating in preventive programmes, to advising on public policy issues. And it suggests that such a strategy is likely to be most effective when those functions are conceived and enacted as *complementary* aspects of an overall plan to tackle both symptoms and causes of crime and disorder, and when in each of them, the police seek to mobilise as fully as possible the active support and resources of local communities and of other agencies for care and order.

But the Handsworth experience also confirms the inherent *limitations* of policing policy in terms of the purpose for which the police service was created: to protect life and property; to control crime; and to keep the peace. It is apparent that public policy decisions in certain spheres, notably those of social and economic policy, are likely to exercise far greater influence over those purposes than policing policy can ever hope to do. On these grounds it clearly becomes essential to consider issues of policing policy in the wider public policy context. Lord Scarman makes the point succinctly: 'the policing problem is only one aspect – though admittedly a vital one – of the social problem and cannot be properly understood in isolation'.[17] Indeed, Lord Scarman's recommendations are as pertinent to Handsworth as they are to Brixton and to other inner city areas where policing and social/economic problems are similarly linked, if not locked together:

> 'I conclude that much could be done to achieve a better co-ordinated and directed attack on inner city problems, and I recommend action to achieve it; I also recommend that local communities must be fully and effectively involved in planning, in the provision of local services, and in the management and financing of specific projects. The private sector and the police must also be more effectively involved in the attempt to tackle inner city problems.'[18]

'Good policing,' Lord Scarman concludes 'will be of no avail, unless we also tackle and eliminate basic flaws in our society.[19]

But what is the nature of these 'basic flaws'? To what extent are they really amenable to 'solutions' in terms of political/ social/economic policy? On this score, the Handsworth experience offers only limited footholes to optimism, for whilst pointing to the need for, and benefits of, strategies on the lines indicated above, it also sharply reminds us not only that the control of crime and disorder lies far less with the police than with society, but also that order, like care, is rooted in the nature and quality of society's structures, relationships and values; and that – failing other motive forces – loss of *communality* in those structures, relationships and values means losses in society's capability to protect life and property, to control crime and to keep the peace.

At the heart of the matter, then, are the trends within our culture. And in an increasingly atomised and mobile society, increasingly dominated by rapid technological change, and increasingly vulnerable to mass consumer values, these trends give scant causes to be sanguine. Despite long traditions of stability in our society, John Donne's vision hovers before us:

> 'Tis all in peeces, all cohaerence gone;
> All just supply, and all Relation:
> Prince, Subject, Father, Sonne, are things forgot,
> For every man alone thinkes he hath got
> To be a Phoenix, and that then can bee
> None of that kinde, of which he is, but hee.
> This is the worlds condition now. . .'
> *An Anatomie of the World: The first anniversarie*
> (1611)

But a measure of pessimism does not invalidate fresh, and more comprehensive, strategies to combat crime and to keep the peace. Indeed, awareness of our vulnerability may spur them on. And amongst the multiple divisions, ambiguities, shades of grey of the Handsworth experience, what is not in doubt is the need to reaffirm, renew and remake the traditions of policing by consent.

Appendix A

Lozells Project
Wallace Lawler Centre
Timetable for centre-based activities
Autumn 1980 – Spring 1981
Monday

Cleaning interior of building 09.00–13.00 hours
Three ladies, complete sweep, wet mop throughout. Kitchen work surfaces. Walls. Waste bins washed out.

Lucas Industries Retirement Club 11.00–15.30 hours +
Art Class. Supervised by Miss Hancox. Twelve to sixteen adults. Drawing, water colour, oils. (Hall)

Unemployed Club 13.00–15.00
Sixteen to twenty-five local youths – mostly male. Pool/Snooker, darts. (Upstairs)

Lozells Youth Club 16.15–18.30 – Junior Section
Forty to eighty-five mixed 8–12 year olds
Small games, table tennis, pool, darts, table football.
5-a-side football, 7-a-side netball, organised by Playcentre Sports.
Staffed mainly by police officers from 'C' Division with voluntary assistance.
(Whole building in use)

Lozells Youth Club 19.30–21.45 – Senior Section
Forty-five to one hundred and twenty plus young people aged

13–17+ mixed in ratio 40 female to 60 male (varies). Activities include –
Table tennis, pool, darts, small games, table football, snooker. Staffed mainly by police with voluntary assistance, and sessional staff from Aston and Handsworth Institute. (Whole building in use)

Tuesday
Cleaning interior of building usually 09.00–13.00 hours
Carried out by cadets. Sweep throughout. Mop as required to clear up spillage/scuff marks. Clear litter round building.

West Midlands Probation & After-Care Service
Two people on community service orders arrive approx. 10.00–10.30 hours to carry out 4–5½ hours work towards their community service order. General cleaning, site clearance, painting, paint cleaning, cleaning mini-buses. Assistance with collection of bulky goods. Digging, weeding, etc. . . Probation Officer maintains contact with centre, through frequent phone calls and regular visits to see clients on site.

Lucas Industries Retirement Clubs
Yoga organised by Mrs M. Page, Co-ordinator for Lucas Industries Social Club. 6–12 ladies 11.00–13.00 hours+. (Upstairs)
Bingo, Bring & Buy, Dressmaking & Soft Toys 11.00–15.30 hours.
Dancing (Hall) group size varies. Forty to one hundred and twenty depending on activity.

Holte School optional games scheme 14.30–15.30 hours
(Upstairs) Pool session supervised by a member of Holte School PE staff. Twelve to sixteen pupils aged 14–17 years.

* *Newtown Youth Choir* Starts 28 April 1981.
Organiser – Mrs A. Gehammer. Age limit 8–12 year olds. Drawn from four surrounding Junior Schools.
16.00–17.30 hours. (Upstairs)

* *Badminton & Indoor Cricket Coaching* (Harry Mitchell Sports Centre, Smethwick)
Organised by Mr M. Jones of Playcentre Sports. Transport by Project vehicle. Departure from Wallace Lawler Centre at 16.00+ returns at 18.45.

* *West Midlands Probation & After-Care Service. Community Service*
17.50. Arrival of ambulance vehicle with Ratcliffe tail lift, driven by volunteer ambulance driver plus two community service order workers. Arrange collection of eleven to seventeen OAPs for Senior Citizens Club who have difficulty walking. Vehicle makes two trips for collection before, and delivery after Senior Citizens Club.

Senior Citizens Club
Forty-five to eighty-five Senior Citizens (some also members of Lucas Industries Social Club) arrive after 18.30 hours. Bingo, Bring & Buy, dancing. Entertainment. Session lasts to 21.30 hours. (Hall)

* *Camping Group*
Six to eighteen members of Senior Youth Club plus three pupils from King Edwards School on Duke of Edinburgh Award Scheme. Camp craft slides, demonstration sessions. Cooking. Hopefully will lead to Duke of Edinburgh Award Scheme during course of '81–'82. Session begins 19.00 hours, closes approx. 21.30 hours. (Upstairs)

Wednesday
09.00–10.30 Cleaning and preparation
Eighteen to twenty-five Wednesdays in the year Lucas Industries run a pre-retirement course at the Wallace Lawler Centre. Usually held on a Wednesday. Courses run 10.00–13.00+ hours. (Lectures in Hall.) Preparation then begins at 08.30 hours. 10.30 – Dressmaking and Soft Toys to 15.30 hours. (Hall)

* *West Midlands Probation & After Care* 10.30 hours
Arrival of community service worker(s) for 4–5½ hours Community service activity.

* *Unemployed Club. Careers Session* 13.00–16.00 hours
Supervised by Mrs Doreen Barwick. One hour pool session
followed by careers guidance. Job Opportunities, contact with
Handsworth Careers Centre for advice. Visits. (Upstairs)

* *Swimming Club*
Operates at Grove Lane Baths, Handsworth. Group from
Junior Youth Club section. Group meets at Wallace Lawler
Centre at 17.30 hours for transport by Project vehicles to
Grove Lane Baths. Swimming session 18.00–19.00 hours.
Return approx. 19.15 hours. Twenty-six to forty-four juniors
aged 7–12 supervised by centre staff. Session coached by Mr
R. Storr, Outreach Worker, Holte School.

Dancing Class
Jonathan and Marie Siggars. A private venture already in
existence when the Centre was taken over. A very active
traditional dancing class. Forty-five to ninety+ 8–13 year olds
in two sessions.
First arrivals at 16.30 hours. Group departs approx 21.30
hours. The group takes part in West Midlands Competition
with very good results.
Also provide OAP entertainment for the Senior Citizens Club.

Thursday
Cleaning building 09.00–13.00 hours. Complete sweep and
wet mop throughout. Three ladies.

* *Unemployed Group* 13.00–15.00 hours
Pool/darts/dominoes. (Recreative session). (Upstairs)

* *Lozells Youth Club* 16.15–18.30 – Junior Section
Forty to eighty-five mixed 8–12 year olds.
Small games, table tennis, pool, darts, table football. 5-a-side
football, 7-a-side netball, organised by Playcentre Sports.
Staffed mainly by police officers from 'C' Division with volun-
tary assistance. (Whole building in use)

* *Lozells Youth Club* 19.30–21.45 – Senior Section
Forty-five to one hundred and twenty plus young people aged
13–17+ mixed in ratio 40 female to 60 male (varies).

Activities include – Table tennis, pool, darts, small games, table football, snooker.

Staffed mainly by police with voluntary assistance, and sessional staff from Aston and Handsworth Institute. (Whole building in use)

Friday
Cleaning building 09.00–10.30 hours
Cadets clean building. (Interior and exterior.)
Preparation for OAP Luncheon Club.

* As of 28 April 1981, Birmingham YOP recreational group will use Activity area facilities for sports – e.g. 5-a-side football. Interior of building 09.30–11.30 hours for table tennis, dominoes, pool, darts *if wet*.

* *Senior Citizens Luncheon Club*
Eleven to twenty-seven OAPs for luncheon. (Hall.) Meals supplied by Holte School kitchens. Served by Centre staff and community service worker on voluntary attachment. Drop in by Social Services/Police Staff.

* *Unemployed Club* 14.00–17.30 hours
Recreation Session. Pool, darts, table tennis in hall after 15.00 hours.
Supervised by Mr M. Edwards and Mr Loganathan. 16–25 unemployed youngsters.

* *Social Services Area 3 Intermediate Treatment Group* (IT)
Supervised by Mr R. Reed (Social Services) and PC T. O'Loughlin (West Midlands Police) 17.30–19.30 hours. One Friday in each month.
Basic support. Pool, snooker, darts, small games, outdoor activities, 5-a-side Unihoc. Additional staff from Probation and After-Care and Social Services Area 3.

One Wednesday in each month the Lozells Project Steering Committee meeting is held upstairs at the Wallace Lawler Centre, approx. 14.15–16.00 hours.

One Tuesday in each month the Project Advisory Committee Meeting is held in the evening 19.30–21.00 hours.

Appendix B

Neighbourhood Policing in West Berlin
Observations during a visit in March 1982

The system of neighbourhood policing in West Berlin derives from a critical revaluation of police organisation and methods in the early 1970s. As in Britain, reported crime, public order and traffic problems had risen rapidly there from the mid-1950s; and as demands on limited police manpower increased, so police turned increasingly to motorised 'fire-brigade' styles of policing. This in turn – again, as in Britain – brought in its train increasing demands from the public for more police on the streets and for closer contact between police and citizens.

From October 1974, the West Berlin police were reorganised with the uniform branch and CID under unified central command (*Landespolizeidirektion*), and in five newly-established *Direktionen* (divisions) comprising 31 *Abschnitts* (sub-divisions). The main objectives of the reorganisation were to increase police presence on the streets, and to improve crime suppression through the greater involvement of the uniform branch. As a result of the reorganisation, more officers and HQ personnel were returned for field duty, and the Berlin police were then able to establish and man 756 foot-beats below the Abschnitt level (722 city beats, 18 water police beats, and 16 mounted police beats). The size of each of the 756 beats was determined by a formula which took into account some fifty factors, particularly the numbers of people in the area, reported crime rates, public order and traffic problems, shopping and leisure facilities, business activities, and other special characteristics (e.g. foreign embassies, concentrations of aliens, etc.). The average size of each beat is 0.5 square kilometres, the biggest being about 2 square kilometres, and the smallest (the Europa shopping centre) approximately 0.1 square kilometres. Each of the beats is assigned to an area foot patrol officer within the *Kommissar* (Inspector) range; and each officer is required to be at least 40 years of age, to have a highly rated confidential report and substantial experience (including at least three year's service as *Polizeihauptmeister* (Senior Sergeant) and to have completed a six-month advanced course prior to the job.

Each officer is responsible for the policing of his own area in ways and at times he himself determines within a 40-hour week frame of reference. His main functions are contact with the public; environmental control; crime suppression; traffic control (including accident prevention); and assistance to other agencies (including registration matters). In fulfilling these functions, he acts not only on his own initiative, but also as a mobiliser of police and public resources to ensure the overall safety and security of his patch, taking a central role when other police units carry out operations on that patch.

Policemen operate from their own Abschnitt, where they have their own desks, large-scale maps of their own areas, and files containing comprehensive information on local people, places and activities. Reports of all incidents and offenders on each beat are also on file, so that each officer can rapidly identify what and where local crime and other problems arise. This is regarded as an important factor by the West Berlin police, since their research shows that 80 per cent of all crimes of medium and minor importance are committed by offenders within five kilometres of their own places of residence.

In terms of crime suppression, the main functions of the beat officer are:

1) to stimulate flows of criminal intelligence from public to police;
2) to provide advice and support for CID activities, including

assisting in searches for wanted and missing persons and for stolen goods;

3) to alert the CID to developments of criminal activity in his area and to suggest local assignments;

4) to provide crime prevention counselling within his area (police research has shown that in 60 per cent of 1,000 cases, citizens took precautions as a result of counselling of that kind);

5) the serving of warrants for arrests.

Preliminary research by the West Berlin police suggests that the delegation of responsibility to individual beat officers has done much both to improve police initiative and effectiveness, and to relate it to public acceptability. Perhaps the most significant statistical evidence relates to street crime offences in West Berlin since 1974. (This includes theft in cars, theft from vending machines, sex offences in public, burglary of building sites, kiosk breaking, summer-house breaking, burglary of one-family and multiple dwellings, burglary of shops and display-windows, factory breaking and robberies.)

Street crimes

Year	*No. of Offences*
1974	58,450
1975	62,230
1976	57,821
1977	56,526
1978	50,293
1979	48,711
1980	51,896

This represents a fall of 11.2% in street crime between the years 1974 and 1980.

I shared the experience of a neighbourhood beat officer in Kreuzberg, a traditional working-class area of West Berlin, now in process of renewal and redevelopment, covered by Abschnitts 52 and 53 within Direktion 5. Kreuzberg has a high population density and major concentrations of foreign residents – 20 per cent in Abschnitt 52, 30 per cent in Abschnitt 53. (Just over a ¼ million foreigners live in West Berlin as a whole – about 12 per cent of the total population of 2.1 million. Half of them are Turks.)

Gerhard Melitz, married, age 53, holds the rank of *Polizei-hauptkommissar*. His beat in Abschnitt 52 (total population 74,000) comprises six or seven streets near Kreuzberg Town Hall, with an estimated population of 2,000. Enthusiastic and committed to his work, Herr Melitz has already served four years on his beat, and looks forward to continuing there until retirement at age 60.

Walking his beat with him leaves no doubts about his acceptability to local people. He is greeted by those of all ages in the most friendly way. Turkish children run up to shake his hand. Old men hail him from across the street. Men and women cross the street to consult him. In all the shops, bars, banks, garages and other businesses we visit, he is plainly welcome. Now in a launderette to reassure the manageress, who has had trouble from tramps. Now in a bar shaking hands with young unemployed Turks amongst the pinball machines (unemployment doubled in Germany during 1981, and young foreigners are particularly at risk). Now asking garage hands to look out for certain stolen cars. (He passes by a sex shop. Sometimes they have a live show, and he doesn't want to embarass the clients.) Now at a coffee and hamburger stall, to tell the woman serving there that he has circulated a description of the man who recently held her up at the point of a gun. And so on round the streets, Herr Melitz consulting, explaining, investigating, contacting – clearly knowing his patch and his people like the back of his hand.

Youth problems are of particular concern to him. Eighty per cent of reported crime in West Berlin is committed by young people under 25; and patterns of youth crime there are similar to those found in North Rhine-Westphalia where recent research established that 33 per cent of reported youth crime is committed by 5 per cent of young offenders. At the time of writing (March 1982) gangs of punks and rockers cause a great deal of damage and create a great deal of fear. Herr Melitz therefore visits a local pub used by punks as a meeting place to make contact with them, talk things over, calm things down.

Problems of squatting are also of major concern in West Berlin as a whole as well as on Herr Melitz's patch, where properties are falling vacant prior to demolition or renovation. (Renovation creates additional difficulties of its own since in its train comes swingeing increases in house rents, exacerbating accommodation problems for poorer families.) As squatting involves the offence of trespass, police are required to take action under the German principle of legality, which leaves them with no discretion in the matter. And action to evict squatters is a frequent trigger for protest, confrontation, political polarisation and violence, with the police as piggies in the middle. In the fourteen and one-half months between December 1980 and the end of February 1982, 150 demonstrations following evictions of squatters led to injuries to 895 West Berlin policemen, involving 3,875 offences.

For the police, the bitter irony is that these squatters do not in themselves represent a significant problem. In March 1982 police records showed that 139 houses in West Berlin were occupied by some 1,200 squatters, most of them students or young migrant workers from other parts of Germany, drawn to West Berlin by its labour shortage, or members of the 'Green Movement'. Apart from a few criminal groups moving from squat to squat, most squatters live in communal peace and in the words of one senior police officer, 'communality of this kind may well represent real hope for our society'.

Yet once the legal requirements for the eviction of squatters have been met, the police have almost no freedom of action. And they know that wherever they have to take on this unenviable and largely unwanted role, they will be liable to attack by conservationists and radical interests, just as they also know that if they seek a softly, softly approach, they will be liable to widespread and bitter criticisms from an increasingly conservative public. (Indeed, this highly emotive issue played a significant part during the West German elections of 1981, when the Social Democrats and their allies were replaced by the Christian Democrats as the party of Government.)

Herr Melitz is therefore punctilious to ensure that evictions from squats are carried out to the letter of the law, and with minimum disturbance. He points out a house recently cleared of squatters prior to demolition. Before police moved in, he made sure that the owner had first made an official complaint against the squatters, was physically present with a demolition order in hand, and had demolition workers standing by to go into immediate action. The police then asked the squatters three times to leave voluntarily. Most did. A few had to be carried out. But for the most part, peace was preserved. And as soon as the squatters left, the demolition workers went to work with their steel ball. And that was that.

Herr Melitz sees his role as contact man between police and community, and his official visiting cards designate him as *Kontactbereichsbeamter* (Contact officer) – KoB for short. The more he involves himself in the community and the more he identifies himself with it, with its welfare and security, the wider and more effective his range of contacts become. He liaises – for example – with the Civil Engineering Department at the Town Hall over broken pavements that cause hazards for pedestrians; with the Housing Officer over neglected premises or falling masonry; with the Gas Board over the marking of street excavations; with building contractors over piles of broken concrete left near places where children play; with the Health Officer over rat-infested premises; with Social Services about old people needing help or support; with shopkeepers over car-parking facilities (in one area he had unnecessary restrictions removed); with schools over the care and control of children, etc.

Many of these activities are not strictly 'police business', but Herr Melitz believes they do much to create public trust and confidence in the police, and to enhance the police image in society.

> 'For instance, I make the point of stretching out my hand and shaking hands with every kid on my beat, because my contact with him might be decisive later in life – when, later on, for example, he's told about this "fucking

snooper", he may say "they're not all that way. I knew a KoB who was very nice and friendly".'

Herr Melitz's place in the community is reinforced by his contacts both with those who make complaints against the police and with victims of crime. As the first to visit complainants, and to talk things over with them, he does much to mollify their attitudes to police; and his visits to victims of crime not only do much to calm and reassure them, but also to improve police–community relations. He also gives advisory talks to those whose homes have been broken into, or who have been robbed, to advise them how to prevent further dangers. In some instances, he himself has fixed preventive devices for them – e.g. window clamps for an old lady living in a ground floor flat who had been robbed several times.

Through his contacts in every corner of the community, and with ears and nose constantly close to the ground, a KoB soon becomes both the servant of the people on his patch and a rich source of criminal intelligence, keeping tabs on offenders, spotting potential offenders, and picking up hints of crime and disorder far more quickly than car patrol officers could do. Much of the information gathered by the KoB is passed on to the CID or to the special plain-clothes squads set up by the West Berlin police to tackle particular categories of crime or to work in particular locales (CID and uniform branch officers work together on these squads, each of twenty men divided into five teams of four, a degree of integration probably unique in West Germany). Examples: a KoB report about a local rash of thefts from cars leads to the arrest of two drug addicts; another report about drug dealing in a youth club leads to the arrest of three or four dealers.

As in other major cities, hard-drug dealing and abuse (mainly of heroin) are a growing concern to the West Berlin police; and increasing numbers of crimes, ranging from shoplifting to break-in offences and robberies, are found to be hard-drug related. About 90 per cent of the major hard-drug dealers that come to police attention are aliens, 60 per cent of them Arabs, 30 per cent of them Turks, though at the time of writing the Turkish connection is tending to diminish as the military Government in Turkey cuts off lines of supply. (A main supply line runs through East Berlin, and the authorities there show little readiness to co-operate to halt this source of infection to the West.)

The involvement of aliens in the drug scene is also a source of hostility between Berliners and the foreigners in their midst ('Them' and 'Us'), and this hostility is exacerbated – especially amongst the youth – by the current context of growing unemployment. Herr Melitz is particularly concerned on this score – he is old enough to know from direct experience what race hatred means – and he takes it upon himself to paint out any racial graffiti he finds on his beat.

Despite – and certainly also because of – the many community problems in which he is involved, Herr Melitz is wholly committed both to his own role and to the KoB system of policing. 'For the public, the police could not have done better than set up the KoB system. And for me, the best thing is that I have sole responsibility for my beat and can act on my own discretion.'

But to what extent is Gerhard Melitz's work representative of the KoB system as a whole? How do his functions compare with those of other KoBs in high and low crime areas and in areas of high and low concentrations of ethnic minority groups in West Berlin? What are the ranges and effects of the networks created by KoBs amongst local communities and with other social agencies in such areas? What is the operational standing of KoBs in the eyes of other police units? By what criteria does police management assess the effectiveness of the KoB system? By what criteria do community groups assess the effectiveness of their KoBs? What problems do KoBs find in reconciling the demands made upon them by the police with the demands made upon them by the community? To what extent are KoBs able to link police effectiveness to public acceptability? These and many other questions remain unanswered at the end of my visit.

Yet first impressions certainly suggest that the KoB system has done much not only to improve relationships between police and community in West Berlin, but also to protect life and property, to prevent and detect crime, and to keep the peace. This has been achieved by devolving police responsibility and accountability to local 'patch' levels, and by giving a new primacy to local contact functions, thus giving considerable reality to the hoary – and all too often empty – rhetoric that 'the most important man is the man on the beat'.

For police in other parts of Europe concerned to improve the quality of their operational contact with the public and their relationships with local communities, the Berlin KoB model is almost certainly of key relevance. As such, it merits further study and more detailed assessment.

Notes

Preface
1 See 'Talking Blues' (The Black Community Speaks About Its Relationship with the Police), AFFOR, 1 Finch Road, Lozells, Birmingham, 1978.
2 Rex, J. and Tomlinson, S. *Colonial Immigrants in a British City: A class analysis*, Routledge and Kegan Paul, 1979.

Chapter 2
3 'Flame' is a publication of the Socialist Workers Party.

Chapter 3
4 'The Highest ideal – Faith and Confidence in a God' (Marcus Garvey) from *The Philosophy and Opinions of Marcus Garvey*, Frank Cass and Co. Ltd, 1967.

Chapter 6
5 Source: Birmingham Careers Office Statistics.
6 Djilas, M. *Montenegro*, Harcourt, Brace and World Inc, New York, 1963.
7 See also Brown, J. *The Unmelting Pot*, Macmillan, 1970.

Chapter 7
8 See also Chapter 9.

Chapter 10
9 Brown, J. *The Skelmersdale Co-ordinated Police Experiment*, Department of Social Policy, Cranfield Institute of Technology, 1981.

10 Knights, Sir P. 'Ultimate Command – The Responsibilities of Chief Constables in the 1980s', *Police Journal*, October–December 1981, Vol. 54, No.4.
11 Bacon, Sir R. 'An Old Hand Looks at the Amalgamations of the 1970s', *Police Journal*, January–March 1982, Vol. 55, No.1.
12 Hadley, R. and McGrath, M. (eds.) *Going Local: Neighbourhood social services*, Bedford Square Press/NCVO, 1981.
13 Brown, J. 'The Social Compact of the Police Service' in *The Police and the Community* (eds. Brown and Howes), Saxon House Press, 1975.
14 *The Brixton Disorders 10–12 April 1981*, Report of an Enquiry by the Rt Hon Lord Scarman, Cmnd 8427, HMSO, November 1981, paras. 8.32–33.
15 Moore, C. and Brown, J. *Community versus Crime*, Bedford Square Press/NCVO, 1981.
16 Naipaul, V.S. *The Middle Passage*, Andre Deutsch, 1962.
17 The Scarman Inquiry, para. 6.2.
18 *Ibid.*, para. 8.44.
19 *Ibid.*, para. 9.4.

Bibliography

AFFOR. 'Talking Blues' (The Black Community Speaks About its Relationship with the Police), 1978.

BACON, SIR R. 'An Old Hand Looks at the Amalgamations of the 1970s', *Police Journal*, January–March 1982, Vol. 55, No. 1.

BROWN, J. *The Skelmersdale Co-ordinated Police Experiment*, Department of Social Policy, Cranfield Institute of Technology, 1981.

BROWN, J. *The Unmelting Pot: An English town and its immigrants*, Macmillan, 1970.

BROWN, J. & HOWES, G. (eds). *The Police and the Community*, Saxon House Press, 1975.

DJILAS, M. *Montenegro*, Harcourt, Brace and World Inc., New York, 1963.

DONNE, J. *An Anatomie of the World: The First Anniversarie*, Nonesuch Press, 1949.

GARVEY, M. *The Philosophy and Opinions of Marcus Garvey*, Frank Cass and Co. Ltd., 1967.

HADLEY, R. & McGRATH, M. (eds). *Going Local: Neighbourhood social services*, Bedford Square Press/NCVO, 1981.

KNIGHTS, SIR P. 'Ultimate Command – The Responsibilities of Chief Constables in the 1980s', *Police Journal*, October–December 1981, Vol. 54, No. 4.

MANPOWER SERVICES COMMISSION. *Returns on Ethnic Unemployment, 1981*, MSC.

MOORE, C. & BROWN, J. *Community versus Crime*, Bedford Square Press/NCVO, 1981.

NAIPAUL, V. S. *The Middle Passage*, Andre Deutsch, 1962.
REX, J. & TOMLINSON, S. *Colonial Immigrants in a British City: A class analysis*, Routledge and Kegan Paul, 1979.
SCARMAN REPORT. *The Brixton Disorders 10–12 April 1981*, Report of an Enquiry by the Rt Hon the Lord Scarman, Cmnd 8427, HMSO, 1981.